The Good Road

The Good Road

The Journey Along a Spiritual Path

Louis F. Kavar

Writers Club Press
San Jose New York Lincoln Shanghai

The Good Road
The Journey Along a Spiritual Path

All Rights Reserved © 2000 by Louis F. Kavar

No part of this book may be reproduced or transmitted in any form or by any means, graphic, electronic, or mechanical, including photocopying, recording, taping, or by any information storage retrieval system, without the permission in writing from the publisher.

Writers Club Press
an imprint of iUniverse.com, Inc.

For information address:
iUniverse.com, Inc.
5220 S 16th, Ste. 200
Lincoln, NE 68512
www.iuniverse.com

Cover photo by Marc Tule. Used with permission.

ISBN: 0-595-14717-8

Printed in the United States of America

*In gratitude for the coyotes:
the house-yotes, pups, and dancing coyotes,
always changing form,
who have scampered into my life
with stories, tricks, challenges and opportunities.
Indeed, coyote magic is powerful medicine.*

Contents

An Introduction to the Good Road xi
Part One: A Map for the Road 1
   Chapter 1:   *The Spiritual Path* 3
   Chapter 2:   *The First Step in Walking the Path* 11
   Chapter 3:   *Staying on the Path* 19
   Chapter 4:   *The Terrain along the Spiritual Path* 40
   Chapter 5:   *Roadblocks on the Spiritual Path* 49
Part Two: Accounts of Travelers Making the Journey 59
   Chapter 6:   *Darlene Begins the Spiritual Journey* 61
   Chapter 7:   *Dwayne: Re-Discovering Self on the Good Road* 71
   Chapter 8:   *Tony: The Process of Inner Healing* 79
   Chapter 9:   *The Story of Marilyn: Further Along on the Journey*   90
   Chapter 10: *Beginning the Journey along the Good Road* 103
About the Author 107
References 109

Acknowledgements

A book is never the enterprise of one individual but depends on the experience, work, and sharing of many others. While this book is based on the lessons learned and shared with countless individuals, I am particularly grateful to those who have assisted in the reading, editing, and preparing the original manuscript: Jon T. Armstrong, Joe Bentley, Franklyn and Patricia Bergen, Lorri D. Carrico, Dane D'Alessandro, Dawn A. Mills, OSB, and Valerie Stark, OSB. Their assistance and support have been invaluable to me. Their friendship has helped to make this part of my life journey a very good road to travel.

Introduction

We were hanging out at my apartment, talking. My Native American friend, Houston, stood in front of the bookshelves looking through the titles. "You have a lot of books about spirituality," Houston remarked. "How come so many people talk about spirituality? What is it, anyway?"

I was somewhat surprised by Houston's question. Given the pride he takes in his heritage, it seemed to me like an odd question. Many people think of Native American cultures as being inherently spiritual. I asked Houston to explain what he meant. "I just don't understand spirituality, or what you mean by it. Just seems like lots of words. Tell me what it is."

I have to agree with Houston. There are times when spirituality just seems like lots of words. The words are often confusing. With all the talk and the variety of books, there is little agreement about what spirituality is. Under the heading of spirituality, people talk about religious experiences; twelve-step programs; readings with tarot cards, crystals, and runes; channeling the spirit of a person long dead; past-life regression; or things as simple as a hike in the mountains.

When many people talk about spirituality, they are usually referring to spiritual experiences. A spiritual experience can come in any form. A spiritual experience could be a time of prayer in a church, synagogue, or temple when you believed God was present with you. Or it could be a time outdoors, while hiking or looking at the stars when you felt connected to nature. Or maybe you had a spiritual experience while reading a book or talking with a friend and you found that you were really inspired. There are many different experiences that people consider "spiritual."

What makes an experience "spiritual" is that it touches our spirit, the core of our being, and empowers us to feel connected to something more than our ordinary awareness. That connection may be to a sense of a Divine Presence, an awareness of the cosmos being alive, or of deep communion with another person. Ordinarily, a religious service is just a ritual; a hike in a canyon is just time outdoors; and a discussion group is just people talking. Each of these things becomes a spiritual experience when our inner-most self is touched by something more than what is evidently present in what we are doing. It's the transcendent dimension of something *"more than"* the activity itself that makes an experience spiritual.

Spirituality is a quality, dimension, or capacity in human life that enables us to live with a transcendent awareness of something *more than* the actual activity we are engaged in. Spirituality begins with the experience of being part of a larger whole or in communion with something greater than ourselves. Spirituality builds on these kinds of experiences to change, shape, or transform our lives with a greater sense of meaning and purpose.

Many people confuse spirituality with spiritual experiences. For some people, the spiritual experience is an end in itself. However, spirituality is much greater than just an isolated experience. After all, spiritual experiences are like other experiences: you can have them and keep them to yourself and it doesn't have to make much difference in the rest of your life. However, when we take spiritual experiences seriously and pay attention to what they mean in our lives, they offer us a greater awareness of our lives and everything else around us. Their real power is that they evoke a greater sense or depth in life itself. Living our lives from this greater sense of depth is what spirituality is really all about.

"It's really about the way you live your life?" Houston asked. "Yep," I replied. "Oh," he said with a dismissive gesture, "That's easy. You either live your life the good way or you don't. Indians always knew that." "I'm sure that's true," I said, smiling to myself.

Living life the good way, or as some Native Americans call it, walking the good road, is what this book is about. It is meant to serve as a basic field guide for the journey along a spiritual path. The path you follow is your own. I share from my experience on a spiritual path but don't assume that anyone else will travel the same path I do. The journey you take on the good road is your own and no one else's.

The road is good not because it's easy. It is a good road because through all the twists and turns, the traveler is brought to a deeper realization of life, its beauty and truth, its wonder and resilience.

This book is divided into two parts. Part One presents an introduction to spirituality, spiritual paths, and basic spiritual practices. Simple exercises are included to help you put into practice the concepts contained in this section. A chapter is also devoted to roadblocks on the spiritual path common in Western culture. The combination of information and exercises is meant to help you chart a spiritual path that is right for your life. Part Two presents the stories of people who are walking their own spiritual paths. These chapters will help to illustrate the concepts contained in Part One. Their progress in the spiritual journey will help you to understand the nuances of your own journey. However, it's important to note that the people presented in Part Two are illustrations and not real individuals. Their stories are composite sketches based on the work I've done assisting others on the good road for the last 20 years. The resemblance to particular individuals is coincidental.

Walking the good road of the spiritual journey is a life long process. It really is about the way we live. The spiritual journey teaches us how to live our lives in union and communion with the goodness of life that can be encountered in everything around us. That's indeed what makes the road "good."

PART ONE

A Map for the Road

Chapter 1

The Spiritual Path

It was a little after 7:00 PM. I had just finished watching the evening news. I turned on the computer and signed on-line to check for e-mail. There was a note from my friend, Tom.

Tom and I began corresponding a few years ago. We discuss by e-mail several issues, including spiritual practices. Tom is Native American, Lakota by heritage. I, of course, am Christian. Both our similarities and differences make for interesting correspondence.

In the context of our discussions, I wasn't really surprised to get this note from him:

> *I consider myself to be a spiritual person and I think you do, too. I also think that we consider each other to be spiritual people. Yet we follow very different paths to spirit. So the question is simply, "what is a spiritual person?" (easy question, not easy answer I think)*

I do agree with Tom's assessment: the question is easy, but the answer is more complex. What is a spiritual person? Is one person more spiritual than another? Aren't all people spiritual?

To answer these questions, I need to take a few steps back and ask another, more basic question: What is spirituality? By understanding more about spirituality itself and how a person *becomes spiritual,* the answer to these other often interwoven questions may become clearer.

Think for a moment about a time in your life you would describe as *spiritual.* Perhaps you were sitting on a beach, watching the waves roll in toward you. Or perhaps you were walking at night, looking up at the stars in the sky. Perhaps you were listening to a piece of classical music or watching a performance of dance. You may have been taking part in a religious service or ritual or in a time of personal prayer or meditation. Or perhaps you were witness to the awesome moment of the birth a child or sat with a person who passed from this life. Stop and recall a moment you consider *spiritual.* What was it like? What was happening?

No matter what the actual event may have been, whether praying the rosary or standing on the rim of the Grand Canyon, spiritual moments have a certain quality about them. Spiritual moments stand out from our ordinary experience of life because somehow, in spiritual moments, we experience a connection with something more than our ordinary experience. During spiritual moments we reach out beyond our day to day life and touch something that we don't really know or understand. Moments are spiritual because in those moments we make a connection with something beyond us.

It is not the thing that we are doing that is spiritual in itself. All of us know that on occasion doing something can be boring or routine. Yet, at another time, doing the very same thing can be alive and rich in meaning. The vitality or richness in meaning that we often call "spiritual" has to do with what happens to us, as individuals, at that moment. In a spiritual moment, we awaken to the possibility of connecting with something that is *more than* the simple action we are doing. In a spiritual moment, we become aware of a kind of union or communion with something *more than* ourselves.

Recall again the spiritual moment you considered earlier. What happened? Words probably don't begin to describe the experience. It was probably as if you experienced yourself as whole or grounded but also pulled into or connected with something more than yourself. It felt good. It felt right.

While there are some people who report that they've never had a spiritual experience, from time to time most people have spiritual moments in life. But having had spiritual moments in life does not mean that a person is following a spiritual path. Instead, following a spiritual path means that the spiritual experiences are such a regular part of our life that they transform our awareness of the course of our lives. To answer Tom's question, a spiritual person is a person who lives with an on-going awareness of the spiritual connections in life. A spiritual person is aware of these connections and attempts to live life based on that awareness. Such a person tries to be in balance and harmony with self, others, and the cosmos.

I was raised in an Eastern European Christian home. My grandparents immigrated to the United States from Eastern Europe. Through family and friends I learned aspects of my ancestors' culture and traditions that fostered my spiritual growth and development. My family, church community, and the customs passed from generation to generation imbued an awareness of the spiritual dimension of life. As a child, I learned prayers to say and rituals from church. Yet, our cultural heritage did not leave spirituality at church. We took blessed, holy water home and sprinkled it ourselves and sometimes drank it. At Easter, foods from which we fasted during Lent were ritually blessed and became our Easter dinner. In late summer, flowers and fruit were blessed and shared in the celebration of other holidays. Through all these customs, I learned that the things in the world around me were sacred, holy, and blessed. They were special reminders of a connection with something alive and real that was greater than I could imagine. These customs and rituals provided me with a sense of connection between myself, others, and the cosmos.

In the late 1600's in France, a foot soldier had a profound spiritual awakening. The event was simple: "…in the winter, seeing a tree stripped of its leaves, and considering that within a little time the leaves would be renewed, and after that the flowers and fruit appear, he received a high view of the providence and power of God, which has never been effaced from his soul." (Lawrence, p.5) The soldier later became known as Brother Lawrence, a lay brother in a French monastery. In a brief collection of letters, Brother Lawrence wrote how his life was transformed by a spiritual awakening. From that simple experience of looking at a tree, Brother Lawrence began to be more and more aware of the spiritual connections in life. He lived his daily life from the awareness of those connections. Because of that awareness, his daily life was transformed. In the collection of letters known as the ***Practice of the Presence of God***, Brother Lawrence wrote about deep experiences of union, communion, and ecstasy that occurred while he performed day-to-day tasks which included scrubbing floors and working in the monastery kitchen. His focus in the midst of day-to-day tasks was to be mindful of God's presence. Brother Lawrence maintained an awareness of the connections on the spiritual dimension of life.

Living with the awareness of life's spiritual connections doesn't just happen. Left to our own, we may have a spiritual experience at one time in our life or a moment of insight at another. These occasional spiritual moments are not the same as living a spiritual life. They don't make us spiritual people. Like any other aspect of life, if we want to grow and develop, an on-going routine is necessary.

For instance, if you want a firm, muscular body, you need to do certain things: exercise regularly; follow a healthy diet; avoid alcohol, cigarettes, and other recreational drugs; and stick to the program. Unless you work out at least three times a week, maintain a healthy diet, and avoid certain things that hurt the body, you won't have a healthy, firm, muscular body. Working out once one week, skipping the next week, exercising four times the following week, and eating pizza, french fries, and gourmet ice cream daily will not make a person physically healthy, firm, and muscular.

In a similar way, to grow spiritually, to really live in the awareness of life's spiritual connections, it is necessary to maintain a regular spiritual program. Maintaining this program is often called walking a spiritual path or following a tradition. Walking a spiritual path requires dedication and commitment. It means that a person puts one foot in front of another day after day and keeps walking. The truth is that following a spiritual path is more work than most people are willing to do. Just as it takes two or three months of working out regularly at a gym to begin to notice real, physical change in our bodies, so too it takes time walking a spiritual path to grow. Like working out in a gym, if you stop and return to a life devoid of exercise, that firm muscle quickly turns to flab.

Today, many people are interested in spirituality and various spiritual paths. Few people actually dedicate themselves to walking a spiritual path. Instead, most people prefer a cafeteria-style, buffet approach to spiritual growth. They try a little Buddhist meditation, then read a book by a New Age writer, maybe attend a seminar on chakras and healing, and return to the church of their youth for holidays. The spiritual buffet glutton will seek out many and diverse experiences for a spiritual "high" like attending an American Indian sweat lodge one week, visiting a New Age channeler the next, and then consult an African Shaman or Santeria priest for spiritual counsel. After a few years, these people have had more spiritual experiences than one can imagine and know about lots of spiritual things. But they are no further along the path to spiritual growth than they were before they started. In fact, many of these people are often worse off because, after all these experiences, they have become confused and skeptical. Their lives are really the same as they were when they started.

I believe that a spiritual path is like a well or cistern that drills deep through the soil and rock of human experience. Each well eventually leads to a vast flowing underground river of spiritual life. The only way to really be refreshed in this river of spiritual life is to plunge the depths of the well. Unfortunately, most people prefer to take a taste from one well after another and never really immerse themselves deeply enough to be fully refreshed.

If each spiritual path is like a well that goes to an underground stream, then it becomes important to use the pulley, rope and bucket designed for that well if you really want to drink the water. The pulley, rope, and bucket are the images, metaphors, and disciplines of a particular spiritual path that enable a person to walk that path.

Fundamentally, I don't believe that one path is better or "more right" than another. In fact, I have deep respect for the richness of the great spiritual paths of human history. At the same time, the images, metaphors and disciplines are usually not interchangeable. In other words, the rope from the Buddhist well may not be the right length to reach the water when lowered through the maze of wonders found in the Jewish Kabbalah.

I do not know of one great spiritual teacher who is able to walk two paths at the same time. However, there are those who, while standing firmly in the context of their own tradition, can savor and appreciate the wisdom of another tradition. Christian writers like Thomas Merton and Anthony DeMello explored Buddhism in this way and Bede Griffiths considered the wealth of Hinduism. None of these spiritual teachers denied the power of their own path. Instead, with feet firmly planted along the path they were walking, they appreciated and savored the truth found elsewhere.

The same is true with my friend, Tom. The wisdom and richness he shares is firmly grounded in his path in the Lakota tradition. His sharing of visions and dreams enriches me, but I will never be Lakota. In a similar way, I appreciate the respect Tom shows in listening to my understanding of call and vocation that is part of my spiritual journey as a Christian minister. But Tom will never be Christian. Perhaps one day I will join him in a sweat lodge or he may share with me the simple meal of the Eucharist and our paths will touch. But each of us walks our own way. The important thing is that we walk and stick to the path.

A classic book on Eastern Christian spirituality, *The Way of the Pilgrim*, underscores the importance of continuing daily on a spiritual path. The book recounts the travels of a wandering Russian monk, a spiritual teacher, whose call, vocation, or vision for life is to wander from place to place. It is in the wandering, the journey, the on-going pilgrimage that the monk learns, and grows, and finds the sacred in each part of life.

What makes a spiritual person? In the end, the spiritual person is one who is committed to being on a journey. That trip, taken day-by-day, will transform the person's life. The road isn't always easy. But those who follow faithfully know the rich refreshment to be found.

AN EXERCISE

At the beginning of this chapter, you were asked to think about a time in your life you would describe as spiritual. It could have been at time you were watching the stars, listening to music, or taking part in a religious service.

Recall again that experience or one like it. After you've taken a few minutes to recall the event as completely as you can, in a notebook or on a piece of paper, write for five minutes about the experience. Don't think about what you're writing. Don't try to organize what you will write. Just put the pen to paper and write whatever comes out. Keep writing for five minutes. After five minutes, stop writing.

What you are doing in this exercise is allowing a stream of consciousness about this event to take shape. Read through what you have written. Don't worry about grammar, spelling, or organization. Read to find out what was important to you about this experience. What strikes you about what you have written? What's missing that you thought was important? What's present that you didn't expect?

It's sometimes helpful to repeat this exercise with other life events. This exercise helps to uncover emotions and thoughts related to an experience that we don't recognize at first.

Chapter 2

The First Step in Walking the Path

Walking a spiritual path is a challenge. Many people begin exploring spirituality when crises in their lives leave them facing questions they can't answer. Life crises include illness, the death of a loved one, recovery from addiction or childhood neglect or abuse, or a deep frustration about the seeming futility of life. At times like these, people often search for answers. Some people look for an up-lifting spiritual experience. Individual spiritual experiences can be renewing and life-enhancing. Ultimately, the long-term answers that satisfy us are more than individual spiritual experiences. The satisfying answers are rooted in deeply personal ways of encountering life and can only be found by walking a daily journey along a spiritual path.

How does one begin walking a spiritual path? History provides us with many examples of people who faithfully journeyed along spiritual paths and found the fulfillment they sought. There is the story of the Buddha, the young prince who sought enlightenment, leaving his palace home and wandering with a small band of followers until he encountered truth. There is also Confucius, whose sage wisdom is passed from generation to generation. There is also the story of Moses, the key figure of the Hebrew Scriptures who journeyed along a spiritual path and formed a community of believers that has endured through the centuries. It is the story of Moses, found in the Hebrew book of Exodus, that will be our example of how to begin our own spiritual journey.

The story of Moses and the Exodus of the people of Israel from Egypt to the Promised Land is a familiar one for many of us. It is the story of the ancient Israelite people, the ancestors of modern day Jews, and their journey from slavery in Egypt to a new way of life as a community with hope.

The slavery these people endured for generations was much more than just physical captivity. The slavery of Egypt had deep psychological and spiritual dimensions. Held captive in Egypt, the ancient Israelites were forced to make bricks. It was their job to build the Egyptian empire. During this forced labor, many lost not only their lives and limbs but also their spirits. For more than four hundred years, the Israelites were told by their captors that they were worthless except for their ability to make bricks and build monuments. Their worth as a race of people was reduced to utilitarian value. They were good for nothing, except forced construction. The Israelites were a people who truly knew deep, long lasting oppression.

When life's only value is utilitarian, all meaning is lost. One's talents, personal abilities and interests don't matter. For the Israelites, making bricks was the only thing that was allowed to matter.

It is not merely that the Israelites were dehumanized by having personal worth taken from their lives. Their oppression went further. Hope for the future was gone. From generation to generation, the people simply made bricks. The belief that something in life could possibly be good was lost to them. Meaning, hope and the belief in the possibility of goodness in life are essential elements of our spiritual lives. The oppression the Israelites endured effectively eradicated all these things. Yes, the slavery of Egypt held the Israelites in complete bondage: physically, psychologically and spiritually.

Moses' job was to take this group of devalued people and forge a new identity for them. That must have been a daunting challenge. How could people who knew only 400 years of slavery actually believe that a new, unknown god had chosen them and would deliver them into a land flowing with milk and honey? What could have sounded more outrageous? They must have wondered if Moses was simply mad. After all, the only thing the Israelites knew was life in the mud pits, making bricks with straw.

After a series of what seem to us like strange and bizarre events, including plagues of locusts and frogs and water turning into blood, the Israelites left Egypt and crossed the Red Sea into the desert. For forty years, they wandered in the desert as they tried to develop a new awareness of themselves. They tried to understand that there was something worthwhile and special about them. All the miraculous stories in the book of Exodus must be read from this perspective if they are to make sense to us today. The God of ancient Israel is presented as the One who would do anything to prove to this people that they had self-worth, that they were cared for and, indeed, chosen.

This time of wandering in the desert made for a long, hard journey. There were times when it seemed they had lost their way. Through the twists and turns of their journey, God was faithful to the people: giving water from the rock; feeding them with manna (a kind of bread that mysteriously appeared each morning); providing a feast of fresh quail; traveling in front of the people as a cloud by day and a pillar of fire at night. Yet, it seemed that on every step of the journey, the people grumbled and complained. At times, they wanted to go back to Egypt, to the land of oppression, and fill themselves with the fresh foods they missed. They wanted what was familiar, what seemed safe and dependable. Their lives of oppression had been very routine and dependable. There were no surprises in Egypt. They made bricks and then they died. Generation after generation, it was the same. The risk of the new journey to a promised land often seemed too great to them. It was too unpredictable; too uncertain.

Many of us have passed through much troubled water in life. At times, friends or loved ones may try to encourage us to keep going. But continuing to walk life's road with hope, believing that there is something good for us in the future, can be overwhelming. Sometimes, life's unexpected events, such as sudden illness or unexpected misfortune, knock hope out of us. More often than not, it is the constant struggles in our lives that seem to deaden the spirit the most. For many of us, the struggles include things such as a history of bad relationships; never quite getting a handle on personal finances; work that doesn't seem to do much else but pay the bills; or the burden of old pains and self-doubts left from scars of things that happened long ago. No matter the reasons, when our spirits are deadened, we look ahead and it all seems hopeless. Our own personal experiences of Egypt, the times when we lose hope and vision, often seem more comfortable and secure than taking the risk on an unknown future. We look at the future and wonder: what if it doesn't work out? Or perhaps we wonder something even scarier: what if it does work out and our heartfelt hopes are fulfilled? What will I do then? Yes, sometimes success is scarier than failure. Whether following our hopes would bring us success or failure, like the Israelites of old, many of us do our best to return to the security of Egypt. We miss the opportunity available to us in the present moment, which is the first step to hope for our future.

Over the years of wandering in the desert, Moses became very disheartened at how long it took the people to understand that there was something good in them and that life had a promising future. He often called them a "stiff-necked people." God, too, often demonstrated frustration at having done so much for the people. No matter what amazing thing God did, the people just didn't get it.

One story in particular recounts just how frustrating for God their lack of vision was. It is found in chapters 32 and 33 of the book of Exodus. God said to Moses, "You are about to enter the land flowing with milk and honey; the land I promised your ancestors that I would give to you." God continued, "Moses, this people is stiff-necked. If I go any further with them, I'll kill them. I'll smite them myself, even though they are my chosen people. I'm over it, big time! So I'll send an angel to clear your path. But I'm out of here!"

In such a time as this, what did Moses say to God when God was ready to give up on the chosen people? Moses reminded God of the commitment God made to stick with the people. Moses also reminded God of the friendship the two of them shared. Moses asked, "Didn't you say that I was your special friend? Didn't you say that I have found favor with you? If that's true, how can you leave now? If you aren't with us when we go into the Promised Land, what will the other nations say?"

In the face of Moses' reminder of the covenant, God recants and agrees to continue on the journey, to stay with the people.

There is an extremely important lesson here for us to remember: our faithfulness to the step-by-step process of spiritual growth does not mean that God will turn bad times into good ones. No, the pain of life is not taken away because we are spiritual. Nor is every difficult experience transformed into a party. The promise of God is to be with us no matter what happens. Through the good times and the bad times, God is with us. That's the heart of the Judeo-Christian spiritual tradition. In the end, this is a foundational belief in all healthy spirituality: that there is something within and around us to sustain us on our journey.

Moses continued his discussion with God. Moses told God, "Yeah, it's been hard for me, too. But you can help and make it easier on me. If I really am your special friend, let me see your face."

In this request, Moses asked God for two things. First, Moses asked to be able to experience the intimate presence of God more fully. Moses wanted to know God as completely as he could. But in this particular moment of crisis, Moses was also asking for understanding. Moses had followed God all these years. Moses had been as faithful as he could. How had this faithfulness paid off? Stiff-necked, troublesome people surrounded him. Nothing was ever good enough for them. They always wanted more.

God reminded Moses that no one could see his face. But God did offer Moses something special. God took Moses and shielded him in the cleft of the rock. God came from behind Moses. As God passed Moses, Moses was able to hear all the wonderful things God had done and feel the security of God's hand shielding him in the cleft of the rock. Once God was past him, the hand of God was pulled away so that Moses could look and see the back of God. In other words, Moses saw God walking ahead of him. Moses then clearly saw where God was leading him. In that moment, Moses saw the spiritual path laid out in front of him. According to that vision, he would take the next step and walk.

Many people struggle, wondering where God can be found, questioning whether spirituality has any worth, or looking for the answers to the problems in their lives. We want the security of knowing what is real and what is an illusion. We want clear answers. But such clarity is not the foundation of living a spiritual life. Living a spiritual life requires that we walk by faith, believing in a presence that supports, nurtures, challenges and sustains us. It is a presence that is always with us.

This story in the life of Moses gives us an example of the kind of faith that is necessary to find the spiritual answers for our lives. The people were very difficult to deal with. Moses often wanted to throw in the towel. Even God was afraid that the Divine anger would flare and deal a deathblow to the people. Yet, God and Moses were faithful to the mission, the vision, and the promise for the future—even when times were very difficult.

Walking a spiritual path requires that we take this example to heart. Instead of struggling for answers, asking questions that simply seem to lead to more questions, we need to stop and be still. We need to go to that quiet, secure place, a place that is like the cleft in a rock, and be enfolded in the Divine Presence. From that holy place, we need to remember the many ways goodness and grace have been present in our life in the past in order to understand all the wonderful things Providence has done in our own lives. When we recall that sacred memory, resting securely in the Presence, we then can look to see the next step on our journey through the eyes of faith. The first step is resting securely and quietly in the presence of God.

AN EXERCISE:

In this exercise, take some time alone to explore the spiritual experiences that are part of your life. Go to a quiet place for a half-hour to an hour. Take with you a notebook or some paper and something to write with.

1. Begin by allowing yourself to be quiet. Say a prayer in your own words to help focus this time. The prayer may go something like this: "Spirit of Life, thank you for this time of quiet. I know you are with me because I am here, alive and breathing. Still my heart and allow my mind to be clear. Guide me and show me the path I am walking. Amen."

2. On one piece of paper, draw a line the length of the paper. At one end of the line, mark your birth. Mark the other end, "Today." Think about your life and note along this line the events you consider most important in your life. Mark them by how old you were when they occurred or by the year they happened. This time-line of your life should contain all the events you consider important in your own life.

3. On a second piece of paper, draw a similar line, marking one end with your birth and the other end "today." On this line, mark the events that you consider "spiritual." These events may be religious or they may be moments of insight. They may be moments of joy or moments of pain. There may or may not be an emotion that you remember. These spiritual moments are times when you found yourself connected to something greater than yourself, something beyond yourself. List as many as you can think of.

4. Compare these two life lines. What do you see? Are there any patterns? Did spiritual moments tend to occur when things in your life as a whole were going well, or poorly, or even when they were mediocre? Were there more spiritual moments at one time of your life than in another? If

so, what other events were happening? What was happening when there were few spiritual moments? Pay attention to all of this.

5.   Like Moses, you have spent time alone understanding the spiritual moments in your life or, as the book of Exodus puts it, hearing where God has been present. When Moses had this experience, he was shielded in the cleft of the rock by God's hand. After he reviewed his life and the spiritual experiences he had, Moses looked out from the cleft in the rock and saw the back of God as God walked in front of him. Like Moses, once you have completed this exercise, it is time to look ahead and understand the next step of your spiritual journey based on the steps you have taken in the past.

Chapter 3

Staying on the Path

November 12, 1986. Miami Beach, Florida. Having completed the presentation of a paper on policy issues for social service providers facing the impact of HIV/AIDS, I left what I believe was the first national social service conference on HIV, The Challenge of AIDS, in search of a quiet spot on the beach. With a towel from the hotel, I spread out on the warm, white sand and savored the beach, the roll of the waves, and the amazing blue sky streaked by white clouds. A smile came to my face as I sipped my diet coke from a plastic mug imprinted with a pink flamingo logo. Once settled in this place, I made an entry in my journal:

> I just did my presentation at the conference. I've done better…. much better, in fact. I felt like I never really connected with the audience. One comment was that I needed a more dynamic style of presentation. How dynamic can you be talking about policy development?
>
> It's been an odd trip for me. Miami isn't what I expected. I don't think I like it here. But sitting here, I feel a draw. I don't know why. It's like there's something special about the place…. Something special here for

me. But, at least right now, I think I'm missing what it is."

As I sat on the beach, recording feelings that just didn't fit with my conference experience, how could I have known my future? I didn't really like Miami from my first visit to the city. But something inside of me gave me a sense that there was something special in Miami for me.

In July of 1987, I returned to Miami Beach for another conference. This time, it was the biennial gathering of the Universal Fellowship of Metropolitan Community Churches. It was at that conference I decided to complete the process of transfer as clergy to this denomination. In July 1987, I thought: "That must have been what I was feeling last year when I was here!"

In time, 1992 arrived. It was April when I packed my home in Pittsburgh and moved to South Florida. For six years, Miami was my home. Miami had been very important in my life. In 1986, I hadn't a clue that I would begin Metropolitan Community Church of South Beach or work with Greater Bethel African Methodist Episcopal Church to help organize a specialized HIV education program in the historic black community of Overtown. While I couldn't have imagined these events in the mid-1980's, somehow inside of me I knew that there was something here for me.

The truth is that my move to South Florida was preceded by bitter reality. Having lived in Pittsburgh for fifteen years, I found that I needed to move from what had become my home. In some ways, I felt that I had outgrown the city. But more pressing was the pain and grief I felt there. Having worked for years with HIV/AIDS, many close friends, some of my best friends, had died. It seemed as though there was no place I could go in the city and not be reminded of what I had lost. Upon the completion of my doctoral dissertation on AIDS related bereavement, I knew that it was time to leave and begin a new life.

My destination became South Florida for several reasons. Suffice it to say that while working at that time for my denomination, my income was such that I could not afford to live in the cities I would have preferred. A colleague of mine in Fort Lauderdale became very persuasive about my coming to South Florida. So, the day came for me to begin my life there.

For six years, I savored the beaches and the ocean breezes; the heavy, humid air; the amazing beauty of ever changing skies; and the wonder of sunsets. Drives through the Everglades replaced long walks in the woods of Western Pennsylvania. Miami gave me a different perspective on life as well as an important time to heal from deep losses and move beyond the pain of grief.

When Moses was crossing the desert with the people, an important event occurred. With the people camped in the desert, Moses went up the mountain to be with God. The cloud shadowed the mountain. On the mountain, Moses encountered a bush that appeared to be burning but was not consumed by the flames. A voice came from the bush and told him, "Moses, take off your shoes. The place you are standing is holy ground."

Remember what Moses' life was really like. He was born at a time when the Egyptians were killing all male Israelite children. Moses was taken from his mother, placed in a basket and set adrift in the river. It was hoped that the child would be found and cared for. He was—by a servant of the Pharaoh's daughter.

Moses was raised in the royal household. In time it became clear that he was not royalty at all. Tension grew between Moses and the ruling class, as he became a defender of his people. He eventually found it necessary to leave the royal palace and live among the Israelite people who were suspect of him because of his royal up-bringing.

Following what must have seemed like a very strange call from God, Moses challenged the Pharaoh and the Egyptian government. This challenge resulted in the exodus of the Israelites from Egypt. After accomplishing what must have seemed impossible, Moses and the

Israelites journeyed in the desert and reclaimed their ancient heritage as a nomadic tribe. But the people fought him every step of the way.

The life of Moses was filled with twists and turns; ups and downs; loss, hardship, difficult times, as well as times of wonder and amazement. All the unlikely events of Moses' life led him one day to go up the mountain to find that burning bush. There he was told to take off his shoes because the place he was standing was holy ground.

In fact, this point in Moses' life was just where he was supposed to be. Moses was where he needed to be. After all the good things and bad things in his life, Moses came to a moment where everything he knew and understood really didn't matter. He was simply present, with all he was and wasn't, to something beyond himself, greater than himself. His past didn't matter. His future was of no concern. In that moment, he encountered something that was simply awe-inspiring. The place on which he stood was holy ground.

As it was with Moses, so it is with us today. As we go through the events of our lives, we don't understand why things happen to us. We wonder if there is a pattern or, perhaps, even a plan. In the course of it all, each of us goes through many difficult, painful moments in life. Fortunate people are the ones for whom the good moments in life outweigh the bad. But, in fact, life is difficult for all of us. Despite all of life's difficulties, the mistakes we ourselves have made, the injustices done to us, and the many disappointments we have suffered, we are here today, simply as the people we are. It is in this moment, just as we are, that we have the opportunity of encountering a Presence that is more than we are, more than our life experiences. In the moments when we encounter that Presence, we need to take off our shoes, yes, out of reverence but also so that we can stay a while. The place where we stand today is holy ground.

Moses didn't just wake up one day and find himself ready to lead the people out of Egypt. Nor did God give him the Ten Commandments the first time Moses had a spiritual experience. It took years for his faith and trust to grow to the point where he could embrace his mission. The more fully Moses' life was transformed by his sense of call, mission, and vocation, the greater the spiritual dimension of his life grew.

The same is true for each of us. It took years for me to make sense of little things in my life, to understand that somehow, something led me onward to places and people I couldn't imagine on my own. In the mid-1980's, sitting on Miami Beach, I knew there was something special for me about the place. I never could have dreamed what it was. It required faith-filled, on-going discernment to see the connection between that feeling and the events of my life. That took time. After all, the great mystic saint of the Middle Ages, Teresa of Avila, wrote that for the first forty years of her life, marked by faithful prayer, was nothing more than mediocrity. It was after mid-life that Theresa's mystical spiritual breakthroughs occurred.

For each of us, learning to believe, trust, listen, hope, and walk the path of our life takes steady discipline and training. Yes, growing in our spiritual lives, taking the steps necessary to really walk a spiritual path, requires that we make spiritual exercises or practices part of our daily lives.

In this section, we will examine four basic spiritual tools (or what are traditionally called "spiritual disciplines" or "spiritual practices") and how these tools assist us on the journey. The four we will examine include journaling; prayer and meditation; spiritual reading; and faith sharing.

Keeping a Journal

Journals can have many purposes. Sometimes a journal is a chronicle of events or a diary. In it, a person records the story of his or her life as it is happening. Journals are also important as psychological tools. Thoughts and emotions that are difficult to express can often be expressed and resolved in the process of writing. Getting the thoughts and feelings out, externalizing them, provides many people a sense of emotional release and resolution. After such a release, some people discover that they are ready to see their lives again from a fresh perspective.

A spiritual journal is something different from a chronicle of events or a written form of emotional release. While spiritual journals may indeed chronicle the events of our lives as well as help us to express emotions, spiritual journals are records of our perception of our spiritual longings and stirrings. In a spiritual journal, a person records the ways in which the Divine presence touches her or his life and moves the person.

The awareness of a spiritual presence in life may be startling, comforting, confrontive, consoling, healing, painful, or disjointed. When we become aware of deeper connections in life, we may be jolted out of our current understanding of life because we see the radical injustice of society. Or we may achieve a new level of understanding of the inter-related complexity of the universe and our part in it. Sometimes, a spiritual insight evokes a response in ways that we never considered before, as it did for Mother Theresa when she first felt the need to care for a dying person in the street. Having served as a teacher for wealthy girls in India, one day Mother Theresa was overcome by the needs of a man dying in the street. Even though her superiors insisted she remain a teacher, doing the things others had depended on her for, Mother Theresa responded to a new sense of vocation which resulted in what has become an international community of sisters and brothers who care for the poorest of the poor. It was the need of one poor dying man that touched the heart of Mother Theresa and called her to a new way of living. Her response to this experience, in turn, transformed the lives of countless other people. In the same way for us, our daily experiences can transform our lives. That transformation usually occurs in gradual ways, but is sometimes radical, as in the case of Mother Theresa. In either case, it is important that we pay attention to the moments in life that touch our hearts. Whatever their impact, it is important for our growth to trace out the lines of our spiritual experiences and to record our responses to them. It is in this way that we can see the patterns of growth and change.

In the beginning of this chapter, I returned to a journal entry from 1986. I had forgotten about the experience that led to making this journal entry until 1995. One evening, while sorting through some books, I came across the journal I used in 1986. I flipped through it quickly and remembered that first trip to Miami. I was quite surprised to read what I wrote because, in 1995, I started a new church. The experience of sensing something important about Miami Beach in 1986 became very clear to me nine years later. It was equally interesting to me to see that the initial discomfort I experienced would grow into the reasons I eventually moved from Miami.

Some time ago, I visited the home of my parents in Western Pennsylvania. One afternoon, my mother asked if I was going to sort out some of my papers in the attic. I wasn't sure what she meant. It turned out that there were several boxes of papers in the attic from my years in college. These were things long forgotten.

In going through the boxes, I came across a folder of material from a workshop I attended when I was about 20 years old. The workshop was called, "Know Thyself!" I have no memory of this workshop. But there were several pages of questions I had dutifully answered about my dreams and aspirations. I carefully re-read these pages. Twenty years after they were written, I was surprised to see that many of the same issues that I struggled with as a young adult were things that marked my current life. There were dreams that had come to fruition and other dreams that remained unfulfilled. I came to see how values of my past carried me through adulthood. It was much more than a trip down memory lane. It was a re-collection of meanings, values, and principles that have been a guiding force for my life.

The importance of journaling is found long-term. A spiritual journal provides a record that enables one to consider the path he or she has traveled in order to understand the present. Reviewing old journals is a way to assess where one has been in order to consider the course ahead. The way we have encountered hopes and disappointments in our past are often the best resources we have for our future. But we often lose resources when they aren't recorded.

Keeping a journal seems like a laborious process for many people. At the time one records a journal, it may seem like nothing more than writing and writing some more. When one is able to consider the record of one's life events in the detail a journal provides, one gains far greater insight into life. A journal is an investment for the future.

The are many self-help books on keeping journals. Perhaps the most noted is the work of Ira Progroff and the program known as the Intensive Journal. Progroff recommends a multi-leveled form of journaling kept in a variety of sections in a binder. While Progroff's model is clearly an ambitious process, those who engage in it are often amazed by the results.

Keeping a spiritual journal is really very simple. One doesn't need to make entries on a daily basis. But it is helpful to write on a regular basis: perhaps one, two or three times a week. The journal itself doesn't need to be a stunning book. Most of the time, I've just used a spiral bound notebook because they are easy for me to write in.

When making an entry into a spiritual journal, it is helpful to answer three simple questions: what happened? What's important to me about it? What does it mean to me?

Using my own journal entry as an example, I answered the questions in this way. What happened was that I spoke at a conference in Miami. What was important about it was that while I was in Miami I felt a sense that it was a place that would be significant to me. I also knew that I both liked and didn't like the city. What it meant to me was that there was something going on here that I didn't understand. I couldn't answer all my questions about my trip at that time, but I knew I could record them to consider them again at another point in my life's journey.

Periodically along life's journey, it is useful to re-read past journals. Specific times to re-read journals include times of transitions, frustration, or loss. At such moments, a person can look back and see how she/he got through difficult moments in the past. Another time it is helpful is when beginning something new: a new project, a new relationship, or a new phase in life. When entering something new, reviewing how I engaged in other "new things" in my past often gives me insight into starting off in an even better way. Finally, there are times when nothing is particularly happening in one's life but it's simply useful to look back and understand where we've been. This is sort of like a New Year's assessment of the past. Perhaps this happens in a formal setting such as when on a retreat. But for most of us, this is something we would probably do on a cold, winter's day when we stay at home and are just in a reflective mood. These times are often the most insightful because we aren't looking for an answer to anything special. Instead, we're simply considering how things have been. When reading old journals in this setting, it's helpful to consider such questions as what things are repeated year after year? Where do I find the most joy or sense of well-being? What things are most frustrating? Are there patterns of any kind? Or do I find a lack of pattern? Most importantly, what do all these things mean to me? How do I understand what I read in the context of my spiritual beliefs?

Keeping a journal is an important spiritual discipline. But it is used best when it is used in "cross-training." Cross-training is when an athlete is trained in another sport in addition to the athlete's own for the training benefit. From this perspective, keeping a spiritual journal will bring the most benefit when used in combination with any of the next three spiritual disciplines: prayer and mediation; spiritual reading; and faith sharing.

AN EXERCISE

This is a simple exercise, but one that you shouldn't skip.

Take a few minutes break from reading to begin a spiritual journal. Keep it simple. Just grab a piece of paper, a notebook, or open a blank screen on your word processor. Think for a moment about what in this chapter or book has struck you. Perhaps it was a new insight. Maybe it was a story. It could have been that reading this book got you thinking about something else important to you. Whatever it was, take five minutes and just write. Don't try to organize or edit it. Just write whatever comes out. See where the thought you're having about reading this book takes you. After five minutes of writing, just pause and re-collect your thoughts. Be sure to save what you've written.

Repeat this exercise several more times as you read this book. I'd recommend taking five minutes to write after you complete each chapter or section. That will be a good beginning to your spiritual journal.

Prayer and Meditation

It was about 8:00 in the evening. I stepped onto the balcony. With book in hand, planning to read I sat down to relax for a while. I looked up and saw the stars flickering in the sky. Looking past the airplanes, I found it. Yes, there it was! Hale-Bopp comet was flickering, wagging his tail in my direction.

A smile came to my face. I enjoyed those quiet evenings with the comet as my companion. I miss his departure. But that night, I enjoyed watching the stream of light in the evening sky.

As I sat, keeping a restful vigil in awe of the small light moving gracefully in the evening sky, the words of Psalm 8 filled my head:

> *When I see the heavens, the work of your hands;*
> *the moon and stars that you arrange,*
> *(I wonder) what are we that you keep us in mind,*
> *mere mortals, that you should care for us?*
> *How great is your name, O Lord God,*
> *in all the earth!*

Comet watching. Gentle rest in the evening. And prayer. I sat in meditative awe and wonder as time passes without notice.

What makes this simple experience prayer?

Often, we think of prayer as asking for something. "God, heal my friend; help this relationship; give me a new job." We're all familiar with those kinds of prayers. While these prayers are often real, heart-felt intercession born in the pain of life, prayer is not about asking for things. At its root, prayer is drawing faith-filled connections among life's experiences.

I sat and looked at the comet. The comet, a purely natural phenomenon, is looked at, studied, and given a variety of meanings by many people. An astronomer studies the comet and draws connections with scientific theory. Lovers, sitting parked in a secluded place, look at the comet and draw connections of romance. Sitting on my balcony, watching the comet, I was drawn to connections of wonder based in my spiritual tradition. Drawing connections with faith or spiritual beliefs is the basis for prayer.

Whether I sit in silent meditation repeating a mantra on my breath, or hope for the healing of a sick friend, or am filled with enthusiasm while singing choruses at the gospel service, I am praying. In prayer, I make connections among my life experience, the object of my focus, and my faith. Repeating the mantra connects my inner experience with the balance I believe holds the cosmos together. Hoping for healing connects my desire for my friend, my friend's need, with a belief in healing. Singing choruses connects my emotions with a community that gathers to celebrate a belief in God's goodness.

There are many techniques used in prayer to help make the connection between our life experience and faith. On a basic level, prayer puts us in touch with a sense of rhythm in life. For instance, American Indians sing to a beating drum. The drum echoes the heartbeat of Mother Earth. Singing and drumming, often a form of prayer, envelops the participants in the rhythm of life in a very direct way.

Chanting, a cornerstone of both Buddhist and Christian spiritual traditions provides the same kind of experience as drumming. In chant, a person's focus is absorbed in a simple melodic pattern and often with words that repeat. By refocusing one's attention with the use of chant, a person's spirit has the opportunity to connect with something greater than simply singing a song.

Today, many people have a similar kind of experience when walking or running. I have often heard runners talk about the way their mind clears while running. Of course, when one runs hard enough, the endorphins kick-in and another kind of high occurs. Unfortunately, most runners don't use their time running as a spiritual exercise. But it can be done.

A friend has repeatedly shared with me that her spiritual discipline is linked to walking along the ocean in the morning. She walks briskly most every morning, using the steady pace of her walk to return to a sense of rhythm and balance. She also uses a mantra or chant to continue this process. For many people, it is important for both the mind and the body to engage in some activity so that the spirit can be free enough to explore.

While many activities can be transformed into a form of prayer, it is important to begin by simply learning to pray. As with any skill, to benefit from the skill, one has to start with the basics and then learn how to adapt them.

I remember when my father tried to teach me how to spade the garden. It was really frustrating for me. The shovel seemed clumsy and awkward. I wanted to just hoe the ground because I knew how to do that. But my father insisted that I use the spade. The hoe did not dig deep enough. To make enough room for the roots, it was necessary to first turn over the ground with the spade, then hoe the larger clods of ground.

My father was an expert gardener. The garden edges were neat and straight. He made them with ease when he spaded the ground. But when I picked up the shovel, I couldn't get it down into the ground. Sometimes I turned over too much ground. Sometimes not enough. My edges were never straight and even. I believe the next-door neighbor used the phrase, "Crooked as a dog's hind leg" to describe my progress. But in time, with practice and real work, sweaty work in the sun, I learned how to use a spade. Eventually, the implement became an extension of my arm. I never had the same ability as my father, but I learned and didn't do a bad job.

This is often the process when we learn anything new. We become frustrated because we don't get it immediately or can't do it as well as someone else. With prayer, people often wonder, "Why isn't it good enough the way I do it?" The truth is that prayer is not unlike spading. You need to take the time to learn to dig deep enough with the shovel for the roots to grow. Then you can use the hoe to break open the larger clods of ground. With prayer, the simple, basic forms need to come first. Then they can be adapted.

Of all the spiritual writers who address prayer, I believe that the work of M. Basil Pennington provides perhaps the clearest and easiest to understand method for prayer. Pennington describes a type of meditation he calls *Centering Prayer* in a book by this title published in 1980 by Doubleday.

Having spent years of research on prayer, Pennington asserts that the most basic forms of prayer can be summarized in a few simple steps. Taking time to master these steps is essential for a good, hearty prayer-life. Centering prayer, sometimes called "centering", is a basic form of meditation.

The process of Centering Prayer can be outlined in four simple steps:

1. At the beginning of the time of prayer, take a few moments to settle yourself. Taking a few deep breaths will be helpful. Sit quietly and simply be still. Open yourself to the Presence that is greater than we are ourselves.
2. After resting a bit and allowing yourself to be quiet, silently repeat a "prayer word" to yourself as you breathe. Keep it a simple word. The prayer word may be a word for God, as you understand the Divine, like Spirit, Jesus, or Creator. Or it may be a word that has importance to you for that time in your life, like love, strength,

healing, hope, or peace. Allow yourself to simply repeat the word. Don't concentrate on it. Simply repeat it.
3. When you become aware of any distracting thoughts, feelings, or sensations, simply return to repeating your prayer word. Distractions will occur. Don't worry about them. Don't focus on them. Don't try to control the distractions. Most people can't control them. Simply return to repeating the prayer word quietly as you breathe.
4. After a period of prayer, perhaps 15 to 20 minutes for beginners, close by praying a familiar prayer, like the Lord's Prayer or the Serenity Prayer. Pray the words slowly and gently as you end this time of Centering.

The beauty of Centering Prayer is its simplicity. It doesn't take anything beside a quiet place and your willingness.

There are many books written about prayer and meditation. Often, beginners find them confusing because they recommend so many different things. As with anything new, keep it simple. Using a form of meditation like Centering Prayer, a person is able to grow as fully as one who attempts spiritual gymnastics with elaborate techniques.

Again, I recommend keeping a journal of your experiences in prayer. What happened? What was important to you while you prayed? What impact did that time of prayer have for you?

Times of prayer and meditation are often quite ordinary. There are periods when it seems like nothing is happening. Many people become discouraged and stop. Continuing through periods that are dry and dull is often important. They are often the time of quiet before a period of growth. It's important to stick with it.

AN EXERCISE

Before reading further, take fifteen minutes to use the Centering Prayer technique described above. Turn back to the four steps outlined in this section and follow them. Give yourself an opportunity to experience this form of prayer.

After you complete fifteen minutes in prayer, repeat the journal exercise from the last section. Take five minutes to write about your experience of Centering Prayer.

Spiritual Reading

Many of us read. We read newspapers, books, letters, signs, advertisements, and magazines. Right now, you are reading. You are reading about spirituality. So this must be spiritual reading. Right? Wrong.

Most of the reading we do is informational reading. We read to learn or to get information. We also read for leisure, like reading a novel or short story. Spiritual reading is a different kind of reading.

When we read to gain information or for leisure, we read to comprehend the words. We want to understand what's being said. Spiritual reading is not concerned about understanding the words. Instead, in spiritual reading, one slowly reads a text to apprehend what meaning the text has for his or her life.

When a person engages in spiritual reading, getting the book read isn't important. Simply reading a few sentences or a paragraph or two is sufficient. Taking time to read and re-read, slowly allowing the words to fill you, encountering the words, ruminating on what is being said, is what spiritual reading is all about.

Usually for spiritual reading, the text read is a sacred text or an inspiring book written by a spiritual teacher. A simple way to do spiritual reading is:

1. Sit in a quiet place, relax, and take a few deep breaths.

2. Having already selected the text, read over it (or a paragraph of it) to get an understanding of what the text is about.
3. Read it a second time, slowly and carefully. Allow the words to sink in. If a word or phrase strikes you, pause to reflect on it. You may want to re-read it several times.
4. Take time to quietly consider what meaning this text has for you.

To further explore spiritual reading, a helpful book is *A Practical Guide to Spiritual Reading*, Susan A. Muto, Dimension Books, 1976. While Muto's work is somewhat dated, she has clearly outlined the process of spiritual reading. She also outlines a spiritual reading program based on Christian literature. Using Muto's process, one can engage in spiritual reading using the literature of any spiritual tradition.

Spiritual reading has a natural connection with keeping a journal. After spending twenty to thirty minutes in spiritual reading, it can be helpful to take five or ten minutes to record the experience. Simply note what the text or passage was that you read; what struck you about it; and what was important to you in the time of spiritual reading.

AN EXERCISE

The best way to understand spiritual reading is to actually do it. The following is a brief text taken from, *The Teaching of Buddha*. Use the above steps to spiritually read this text:

> *It is a very good deed to cast away greed and to cherish a mind of charity. It is still better to keep one's mind intent on respecting the Noble Path.*
>
> *One should get rid of a selfish mind and replace it with a mind that is earnest to help others. An act to make another happy inspires the other to make still another happy, and so happiness is born from such an act.*

> *Thousands of candles can be lighted from a single candle, and the life of the candle will not be shortened. Happiness never decreases by being shared.*

As with the exercise on Centering Prayer, after you have completed this exercise in spiritual reading, take five minutes to write in your journal about the experience. Write whatever comes to mind. There is no right or wrong way to keep a journal. Don't try to organize it or edit it ahead of time. Just allow the words to flow out onto the paper.

Faith Sharing

Talking about one's spiritual life with others on a similar path is another important tool for spiritual growth. As vital as this tool can be, it's often neglected and under utilized.

We tend to think of our spirituality as something deeply personal. And it is. However, spiritual depth rarely happens in isolation. Left on our own, we can easily lose our way and get sidetracked along the spiritual path.

In recent years, it has been popular to seek out spiritual teachers. Teachers can be of vital importance in developing a healthy, integrated spiritual life. Great spiritual traditions have developed specific roles for teachers. These roles are generally accompanied with great respect.

Unfortunately, there are those who freely call themselves spiritual teachers who are nothing more than charlatans. They often snatch onto spiritual sounding words and maintain a warm and inviting profile, encouraging others to follow them. Following them often includes buying their books and tapes and paying for their services. While some of these teachers impart some truth to others, they are generally doing nothing more than fostering a cult around their own ego. Their effect on people is often disastrous.

Why do people fall for these spiritual charlatans? Many people authentically want to know how to make sense of their lives from a spiritual perspective. These false teachers are often very accessible to the public through regular advertising, high profile seminars, and other promotional tactics.

Spiritual charlatans can be found using every imaginable spiritual tradition and practice. They generally expect strict following of their teaching for guaranteed spiritual growth as well as significant payment for their services. Many even have a spiritual sounding reason as to why money is due them, frequently stating that financial success is a sign of God's favor with them. Beware.

When looking for a spiritual teacher, it is important to be an educated consumer. Learn the role of a spiritual teacher in a particular tradition you follow. For Christians, completing degrees or certificate programs in the Christian form of spiritual teaching, called spiritual direction, is a formal credential to look for. Authentic American Indian teachers follow tradition as handed from one teacher to another. Buddhists pass their teaching and tradition by affiliation with monasteries. Jews study under Rabbis, the title itself meaning teacher. Jewish teachers of the Kabbalah have a strict tradition on how this spiritual heritage is passed to others. The same is true for the Sufi Order, a mystical branch of Islam. When looking for a spiritual teacher, be clear to ask the person to identify how the person was trained. Does their training fit within the tradition they represent? Do they have the appropriate background to know what they are doing?

Further, when exploring work with a spiritual teacher, ask the teacher about her or his own spiritual life. There may be a reluctance to share certain specifics, like experiences of dreams or visions. That is appropriate. Spiritual teachers should tell inquirers how they pray, meditate, and follow their spiritual path. If the spiritual teacher doesn't seem to have an on-going spiritual path, or if the person studied it on his or her own without the benefit of a teacher or some other program to give form to their spiritual life, the person probably is not a good teacher.

Untold damage is done to people who follow bad spiritual teachers. People are often preyed on in times of difficulty for their life savings or are forced to give up family and friends for some sort of privileged spiritual insight. Teachers who are doing nothing more than drawing others to their ego sometimes lead people to their death. Many of these spiritual charlatans are expert at what they do. They are con artists and manipulators.

It is important to meet with a spiritual teacher to be sure the person is someone you can work with. Just because the person is spiritual doesn't mean you'll find the person easy to talk to. Identify a teacher who is on a spiritual path you want for your own life. Interview the teacher and get to know something about him or her.

A good teacher will work to empower your growth. There are times when you may find yourself challenged. But ultimately, you will know that the decisions are always yours. This freedom is an important sign of the validity of the teacher. A good teacher will not criticize or condemn you for not following a lesson.

Often, the best spiritual teachers are the ones who are reluctant to accept the title. They see themselves as just another person on the spiritual journey. They know that it has only been through dedicated work and effort that spiritual growth has happened for them. And they know it is a struggle, even after many years. Such teachers are the ones with real wisdom to share.

Spiritual teachers are not the only source of faith sharing. Being part of an informal group that meets periodically to discuss spiritual things can be very helpful. These groups come in many forms ranging from a well-led Bible study at a local church to a monthly coffee with a few friends who discuss a spiritual book together. Simply talking about one's spiritual life with a trusted friend helps each of us to understand our spiritual journey and maintain our walk along the path.

Spiritual experiences often make us feel isolated. After all, people just normally don't talk about them. But having a context to share the journey helps us to understand that we don't walk the path alone; that others have similar experiences; that at times, another has gotten beyond the same experience of dryness or the same experience of being confronted by an insight. Sharing with others keeps our feet on the ground as we walk our spiritual path.

There are many other spiritual tools or practices. As a person progresses along a spiritual path, some other spiritual tools can be helpful, like retreats, fasting, or vision quests. For most on the journey, the practices of journaling, prayer and meditation, spiritual reading, and faith sharing will enable a person to travel the spiritual path in a safe and balanced manner. These spiritual practices are the basics. When we do the basics well, there is a solid foundation built for the future.

AN EXERCISE

Walking a spiritual path can never truly be done alone. Yet, talking with others about our spiritual journey and experiences is often awkward and uncomfortable when this kind of conversation is new to a person. Talking with others about these personal experiences makes many people feel vulnerable. We wonder if the other person will think that we are strange in some way.

In this exercise, I encourage you to talk with someone about your spiritual journey. Realizing this may be uncomfortable for you, there are some ways that may make it easier. Perhaps you can meet and talk with a friend about reading this book. Begin the conversation sharing an insight from the book and let the conversation go from there. If you're uncomfortable talking with a friend, visit a spiritual bookstore or meditation group where you can meet someone to talk to who is already following a spiritual path. That person's path may be very different from your own. That's okay. For now, just learn to talk about your spiritual journey. Another option would be to join a conversation about spirituality in an on-line chat room or post a personal experience on an on-line bulletin board. You'll be able to be anonymous by doing this on-line. You also will be introduced to a wide variety of perspectives this way.

Sharing your spiritual journey with another person will greatly help to make sense of the path you're traveling.

Chapter 4
The Terrain along the Spiritual Path

In the late 1970's, I was a graduate student at the Institute of Formative Spirituality at Duquesne University in Pittsburgh, PA. It was there that I studied some of the great writers of the Christian spiritual tradition. Among them were European mystics from the Middle Ages who used a common paradigm for the process of spiritual growth. This paradigm is a dialectic between *consolation* and *desolation.*

Consolation refers to times when the journey along the spiritual path feels really good, exciting, fruitful, and rewarding. Desolation refers to the times when it's rough, painful, or dry and empty. As I look back at studying the writers who expounded on consolation and desolation, I find it amusing. All they really needed to say was that some times it's easy and some times it's rough. The easy times can be really great. The rough times can be very rough. But whether the journey along the spiritual path is easy or rough, the important thing is to stay on the journey.

Saying that sometimes the road is easy and sometimes rough doesn't prepare the traveler for what may be encountered on the spiritual path. What can a person reasonably expect when walking a spiritual path? How does a person know he or she is covering any ground on the journey? How do you know when you've strayed off the path or totally lost your way? Can it still be a good road when it's rough and rugged?

In this chapter, I'd like to consider six different kinds of terrain that people generally cross on their spiritual path. These different kinds of terrain are described in a variety of ways in various spiritual traditions. In traveling the good road, these different terrains are not encountered in any special order. Instead, walking a spiritual path, one can reasonably expect to encounter them from time to time. The more quickly a traveler learns to recognize these different kinds of terrain, the more steady the journey on the good road will be.

Scaling the Heights

Whether through a conscious decision or by circumstance, a person begins to walk a spiritual path. Sometimes, it happens by association with others. Sometimes, it's the result of an eye-opening, consciousness-raising experience. Sometimes, it's an outgrowth of curious searching for something more in life. Many things bring people to this point. It's at this point that a person simply begins to walk a spiritual path.

In working with both individuals and groups, I have witnessed people arriving at this starting place when I've been teaching centering prayer or other forms of meditation. As an ordained minister, I know that at times people experience a religious service or ritual in such a profound way that it starts them on the path. At other times, people have asked to speak to me about an experience they had of spiritual awakening and their desire to explore this dimension of life more fully. What happens when a person begins exploring a spiritual path?

Often the first experience is one of scaling new heights. Many people are excited, energized, and enthused about a newfound dimension in life. Some can't seem to get enough of this feeling. This positive beginning usually includes increased physical energy; a sense of peace and well being; and a new perspective on life. Less frequently, individuals experience a sense of purpose or direction in their lives. They may experience a new sense of wholeness that was previously absent from their lives. For many people, the beginning is an emotional and insightful awakening. It often is like being "born-again."

Those who climb these spiritual heights are often greatly motivated. The reason for that is simple: it feels good. Since it feels good, they want to learn as much as they can and engage in every spiritual endeavor available to them.

During this emotional high, walking a spiritual path seems quite easy. A person just doesn't understand why everyone wouldn't want to experience this newfound dimension of life. The enthusiasm can often be amazing.

Not everyone encounters emotional energy when beginning the spiritual journey. For a significant number of people, starting to walk a spiritual path is much less dramatic. For instance, I've often found when teaching centering prayer in a group or leading a group in a guided meditation, while most of the group will report something energizing, a few people will have an odd, quiet look on their faces. It's clear that they had a different experience from the others. For them, the experience was much subtler. Some people report feeling quiet inside, but not much more than that.

This lack of enthusiasm is often uncomfortable to people who experience it, especially when others share their rousing experiences. Some of the people who have a quieter experience find the courage to ask, "What did I do wrong?" They didn't do anything wrong. Their experience was simply different from the experience of others. Some people just don't say much about their experience. Perhaps, there wasn't much difference for them before, during, and after the time of meditation.

Those who don't experience the kind of elation that others have with initial spiritual experiences often give up thinking, "This stuff doesn't work for me. I just don't get it." That conclusion may not be accurate. Our responses to walking a spiritual path are consonant with our personality. Those who tend to be more effusive emotionally will often be less restrained emotionally when it comes to spirituality. Those who tend to be more thoughtful may find that spiritual insights are subtler for them.

People with subtle experiences may be tempted to give up on the spiritual path entirely. They simply conclude that there's nothing in it for them. Often, people with quieter experience who continue to pursue the spiritual journey find that the spiritual life has rewards for them in providing insight and understanding from a different dimension.

For those whose initial experience of the good road is marked by a pleasurable kind of high, it should be remembered that real progress along a spiritual path is not measured by good feelings. They are great experiences. But they comprise just one aspect of the journey along a spiritual path.

Pushing Through the Desert

After one has traveled the good road long enough, a traveler will eventually encounter a part of the road that is very dry. It's sometimes referred to as, "a desert experience." The desert is the experience of nothing happening. It's empty. During dry times, a person tries to pray, meditate, engage in spiritual reading, journal, and do everything else that is part of the spiritual path. But no matter what the person does, the path seems arid, dry, and barren.

The desert can last a couple days or a couple weeks, or even longer. The first time a person encounters one, it's very confusing. The person wonders what happened. "Did God abandon me? Was it all a phony experience? Was I just fooling myself?" These are common questions people ask themselves while trying to push through the desert.

Dry periods are more difficult for those whose spiritual experiences have previously been pleasurable and marked by enthusiasm. In the desert, it just feels like the bottom fell out and there's really nothing there.

It's important to pay attention while pushing through the dry parts of the spiritual journey. Crossing the desert with care and attention is of vital importance. Care and attention may take the form of journaling during this dryness. Pushing through the desert often falls into a kind of pattern. One may enter the desert following a particularly intense emotional time. Or the desert may be a precursor to a more difficult period or a period of marked growth. Learning the terrain of the deserts of our own spiritual paths is the most helpful task. Don't try to change them or make them go away. They are there for a reason. Listen carefully and learn to understand the reason.

Crossing the Flat Grassy Plain

Much of the time while walking the good road, there isn't much happening at all. It's a lot like crossing a flat grassy plain where there's nothing to see in any direction but more of the same thing. Many spiritual writers have referred to this as the experience of mediocrity. The flat grassy plain becomes the regular, day-to-day experience of walking the spiritual path after a person has been on the road for some time.

A person crosses the flat plain while engaged in the spiritual journey and follows a routine of spiritual exercises. There are no great heights to scale or rough terrain to cross. Instead, a person continues to continue to walk the path. It isn't bad and it isn't good. It just is.

The journey across the flat grassy plane is sort of the maintenance time. There are no great leaps in growth. Nor are there major stumbling blocks. Growth is measured over time in "just noticeable differences."

In thinking about this aspect of the spiritual life, I often remember the question asked of the Buddha about what happens after Enlightenment. To paraphrase the story, the Buddha remarked, "Before Enlightenment, I drew water from the well and I chopped wood. After Enlightenment, I drew water from the well and I chopped wood." In other words, even for the most spiritually enlightened people, life simply goes on in its usual, day-to-day ways.

The flat grassy plain may also be a kind of plateau. After having explored the spiritual life to a certain extent, the lessons learned from the exploration are integrated into one's life. Living the rhythm of integration is what a plateau is really about. It's actually a pretty good place to be. It's the moment marked stability, balance and equity.

Delving into the Deep, Rocky Crevices

One of the most surprising experiences for people on the spiritual journey is the amount of pain they sometimes experience. Often, people aren't prepared for the pain because they associate a spiritual path with peace, joy and blissful happiness. Yet, pain is very much part of the process. Where does the pain come from?

Spiritual tools or practices have a primary purpose to help us delve into our inner experience. Take, for example, prayer and meditation. With centering prayer or meditation, a person stops everything else to simply be present to what's inside. While many of us believe that what is inside is God or some expression of the Divine, there are other things inside us as well.

Over the time of their life span, many people have built up pain and scars from wounds that are sometimes too deep to imagine. By stopping and being present to what is deeply inside of us, we have the opportunity to explore and heal those painful wounds. These wounds may be the result of childhood neglect or abuse, of economic deprivation, addictions, deep-seated personal fears, crippled self-esteem, unresolved grief, and most anything else in life that has hurt us in some way.

Sometimes, for our own psychic safety and survival, these wounds are buried deeply within us and walled-off from our memory. This is called *dissociation*. The painful experience is dissociated from our day-to-day life and memory. For some people, there are blank periods of memory because entire sections of life were too painful and needed to be put aside in order to survive.

Through the process of meditation, journaling, faith sharing, and other spiritual practices, a person bores more deeply into his or her inner experience. Delving into these inner experiences sometime leads us to rocky crevices. In these crevices we discover fragmented, painful, and scarred emotions hiding between the rocks. Stumbling into these old hurts often catches us by surprise. It's often very painful.

What is happening is that by using spiritual practices correctly a person is boring deeper into his or her inner experience. Sometimes the result is digging up old emotional wounds that have been covered over by layers of scar tissue. Delving into those wounds is painful. But it is only by re-opening the wounds that the pain can be released and healing occur.

Often, when a person encounters pain, the response is to flee. That's an important survival response. If a person continues to push this pain away instead of exploring the pain, healing will be more difficult. Avoiding the pain often results in increased psychological (and sometimes physical) distress.

Delving into the rocky crevices where pain has been long hidden sometimes requires working with a spiritual teacher or mental health professional. In other cases, the pain is such that a person is able to work through it him or herself. The important thing is to work through it and not push it aside.

Along the spiritual path, a different kind of pain may also be experienced. This second kind of pain is more common when a person is further along the spiritual path. While it feels a lot like the rocky crevices in one's own life, it's really bigger than that. At times, an individual may experience intently the pain of the world. In this case, a person may find his or herself overwhelmed by the pain others experience because of injustice or the pain of Mother Earth because of our lack of care for her. This experience is very real and is a sign of living in greater connection with life that is greater than our own lives. It is an experience of great empathy and compassion. Because the spiritual path leads to a deep and real connection with the life of others or the life of the cosmos, those who travel the path long enough will discover the rocky crevices of the world's pain.

The experience of pain draws our attention to specific wounds. It is vital that we give our attention to those wounds so that healing can occur. Perhaps there is no more important dimension of the spiritual journey than moving toward healing and wholeness.

Stumbling into Potholes

Even along the good road, there are potholes. Potholes, those craters that seem to open along the road out of nowhere, break our stride. Sometime, potholes are big enough to fall into. Other times, potholes are small enough to swerve around and miss.

Potholes are the moments of struggle, resistance, or intense emotions, like anger, that seem to draw us off our course along the spiritual path. Potholes are very important. They command our attention. The bump in the road jars us. Often, we're annoyed because the road was smooth and easy to travel, except for the pothole. The pothole may be a signal that something is unresolved for us. It may be there to get us to pay attention to something we'd rather not deal with. And sometimes, potholes are nothing more than distractions.

The two times potholes are most important are when we keep hitting the same one over and over again or when we really get stuck in one. In both cases, there's something that we need to change about how we're traveling the good road. These potholes are clear indications that we're not walking in a way that is right for that part of the path.

Most people on the spiritual path prefer to ignore potholes. They want the road to be smooth. However, we learn more from the potholes than from a smooth, easy road. Potholes are real occasions for growth along the good road.

Gliding over Smooth, Level Ground

After crossing the desert or delving into deep, rocky crevices, a person on the spiritual path often finds him or herself gliding over smooth, level ground. The dryness or pain resolves. That resolution takes a person to a new section of the path where it's smooth and easy.

Gliding over smooth, level ground is another step toward personal integration. It's a time of renewal based on an insight or emotional resolution. The smooth, level ground is where the pain of an old wound is healed; when a person reaches a new understanding or sees a problem or concern in life from a new perspective; or when a person experiences some new dimension to his or her spiritual life, like identifying in some deep way with the experience of another.

In some ways, gliding over smooth, level ground is similar to scaling the heights. A person feels a great deal of energy much like when starting the spiritual path. Perhaps that's because when one is gliding over smooth, level ground there's a sense that the effort is worthwhile because it is resulting in growth.

The journey along a spiritual path takes us across many different types of terrain. It's important to identify the different kinds of geography on the good road in order to navigate them. In doing so we understand what kind of territory we are going through and benefit from them the journey.

Through reflection, journaling, and faith sharing, an individual develops an awareness of these different terrains and how they manifest themselves on the spiritual path. Learning how to walk through each terrain, attending to it and not hurrying along the journey makes for sustained strides along the good road.

Chapter 5

Roadblocks on the Spiritual Path

Most people have spiritual experiences from time to time in their lives. Many people learn to pray meditate, journal, or engage in many other spiritual exercises. Given that many people have the basic experience and tools to proceed on a spiritual path, why are so many people not further along the spiritual path? If people have had spiritual experiences, if they've learned how to use the tools, why aren't they making their way further along a spiritual path?

The answer to these questions is really quite simple: walking a spiritual path takes time and discipline. It requires a commitment. It doesn't just happen. Most people just don't put in the work required for authentic spiritual growth.

I often compare spiritual growth to working out in a gym. In order for a person to show physical improvement by working out, a person must learn to use the equipment, get into a routine of working out at least three times a week and combine weight lifting with aerobic activity. Doing these things and eating a balanced diet will result in changes in one's body. The first real changes will be noticed in about three months. In other words, getting in shape takes discipline and commitment. The spiritual life requires nothing less.

Spiritual growth and development is more difficult for us than other pursuits because spiritual growth is often at odds with the trends and values of society. There is an energy in every culture that seems to pulsate just under the surface of the culture. These cultural pulsations provide the members of that culture a shared context of meaning about life. What are the pulsations in American culture that form road blocks on the spiritual path? In this chapter, four of these cultural roadblocks will be explored.

The First Roadblock: The Instant Society

Microwave ovens. Fast food. Real-time chat on the Internet. Overnight express delivery. Time in our culture is fast, and getting faster. There is a kind of urgency in everything we do. Whether work or leisure, meals or conversation, no matter what it is, we want it fast. Time is very important to us. The faster things can be done the better.

Waiting at stoplights is an annoyance. Someone driving too slowly in front of us brings a response of rage. Standing in line at the grocery checkout, post office, or airline counter is an annoying waste of time. Time is of the essence.

In this rushed way of life, taking time to sit, be still, and focus on the spiritual life seems like an absurdity. Yet, stopping, taking time, and being quiet is absolutely necessary for spiritual growth. Perhaps nothing else is more difficult for people today.

Each of the spiritual exercises discussed in this text requires time: time to slow down, relax, and be still. Spiritual reading requires slow, thoughtful reflection to allow the words of a text to ruminate in our hearts. Faith sharing requires a relaxed, personal conversation. Centering prayer or meditation necessitates sitting in silence for what seems like a long time doing nothing in particular. Learning to stop, take time, and be still in our fast paced world is probably the biggest roadblock on the spiritual path.

Unless a person takes time for spiritual practices and does so leisurely on a regular basis, progress along a spiritual path won't happen. To walk a spiritual path in American culture today really does require climbing the hurdle of a fast-paced life to learn to calm oneself and be quiet inside. Often, the only way over the hurdle is to just take the time and do it. It's by regularly taking the leisure time to be quiet inside that progress toward inner stillness can occur.

The Second Roadblock: Externalized Values

The clothes you wear; the car you drive; the location of your home: these are important measures of personal worth in our society.

Walk into any major department store. A brief inspection of any clothing department is a reminder of how designer conscious our culture has become. The value of clothing has far less to do with its comfort, functionality, or quality. Instead, clothing is valued by the name of the designer found on it. Depending on one's social status and the image one wants to convey, certain designers are "in" while other designers are "out." It's as though the clothing a person wears is a statement about the content of his or her character.

Automobiles are much the same way. Cars are designed and sold for the image they convey. The make and model of a car discloses certain vital indicators about a person: his or her success and value. But isn't an automobile really just a mode of transportation? Don't they all wear out over time? Yet, drivers of certain vehicles are often perceived as different, better or worse, than drivers of another vehicle.

In America, and I am sure in many other places, a person's address says something about them. Growing up in a rural town in Western Pennsylvania, my mother tells of childhood friends, distinguishing among those who lived "front town" and those from "back town." Front town was where "the Americans" lived; back town was home for the Eastern European immigrants.

Urban African-American communities in this country often grew-up around the railroad tracks. In some areas, the railroad separated black from white communities. In Florida, African-American communities grew up along the tracks because they were the laborers who build Henry Flagler's railroad, which has spanned the east coast of Florida for more than a century.

Such trends continue today. In cities across the country, walls and gates separate one community from another. There is the not-so-subtle implication that the gates and walls, while designed as security measures, mark those living inside as among the "have's" as opposed to the "have-not's." Fundamentally, there is nothing intrinsically wrong with clothes, cars, living in one neighborhood or another, or belonging to one social club or another. That is, there is nothing intrinsically wrong when we simply see them for what they are: clothes, cars, homes, clubs, and so forth. The problem is the under-lying belief that people who wear certain clothes, drive certain cars, live in certain neighborhoods, attend certain houses of worship, belong to certain clubs, graduate from certain schools are somehow better than others. These classist beliefs prevent us from realizing our shared humanity.

The externalized values that grow out of classism pose another roadblock on the path of the spiritual journey. First, it is tempting to project these same values onto spirituality. This results in a certain kind of arrogance about one's spiritual experiences or purported spiritual abilities. A person who pays a substantial fee for a guided spiritual experience may falsely believe that the experience is something better than the person who attends a church where singing repetitive choruses and emotional preaching is the style. The externalized values common in our society can also suggest that certain spiritual practices or spiritual paths are better than others. It's almost as though there is a designer-appeal to certain kinds of spiritual experiences: those that are well-packaged, marketed, and somewhat obscure must provide a better spiritual high than those generically packaged and more readily available. The truth about spirituality is that every person is on a path, making his or her way. As soon as a people begin to think they are better or further along than others are, they've probably lost their way.

Secondly, a focus on externalized values fails to respect the value of life itself we each share with all humanity and other creatures. Spirituality is focused on making connections with our life experience and a context of meaning that is greater than we are in ourselves. Spirituality's focus is a dimension that is *more than* what is apparent in our day-to-day reality. How can we encounter this reality when we are not open to experience the truth of life around us because our attention is limited on external issues? Life doesn't come with a designer label. Life simply is the way it is.

Authentic spiritual growth and development require that we set aside these externalized values in order to encounter a different level of truth. Just as the Buddha had to leave his secure life in the palace and live among ordinary people before achieving Enlightenment, so we, too, need to step beyond the limitations of class-consciousness to walk our spiritual paths.

The Third Roadblock: Consumerism

Related to externalized values is the consumerism found in our culture. Actually, externalized values are intertwined with consumerism. One goes with the other.

In our culture, we've been implicitly taught that our personal value is based on what we own. The more we own the better people we must be. Marketing plays into this belief and reinforces our self-perception that we really aren't good enough unless we have the newest, the latest, and the most expensive things available.

To help fuel this cycle, obsolescence is built into most manufactured goods to assure that after a period of time we will be forced to buy a new product. Products are guaranteed to wear out and break. They are simply designed that way. One example of this is found in the computer industry. Within less than a year, the newest personal computer is considered old technology. Isn't it possible to design a more friendly up-gradable computer for real technological advances? Another example is the automobile industry. Automobile engineers are capable of building cars that could last ten to fifteen years under normal conditions. But if they did, the auto industry would suffer greatly.

Through no fault of our own, we are caught in an endless cycle of buying new products to replace other items designed not to last. We are implicitly taught to believe that our value as people is based on having these latest items. Untold harm is done to people's self-esteem and self-concept because they cannot meet these standards. Consider the frustrations of parents who try to keep up with buying their children the latest toy, game, or athletic shoes because children have learned to believe that they "have to have them." If money isn't available for these things, children often experience distress because they don't fit in with their friends who have the latest, newest, and best items. Our culture teaches the lessons of consumerism at a very young age.

It is difficult for many people not to apply this same unbridled consumerism to spirituality. When many people begin to explore spirituality, having spiritual experiences often becomes the most important issue for many. Using this meditation technique, hearing that speaker, or reaching a new form of ecstasy becomes the driving force behind many people's spiritual lives. The quest for experiences does not result in authentic spiritual growth. If spiritual growth is like working out at a gym, then the consumer driven quest for spiritual experiences is like taking steroids for bodybuilding. Taking steroids results in quick bulk. Stop the drugs and the muscle is gone. Further, the drugs themselves result in many health-related complications. A consumer driven quest for spiritual experiences is much the same. It will provide intense experiences that fade quickly. Ultimately, it will leave a person feeling more insecure about him or herself and less integrated from a holistic perspective than never having had a spiritual experience in the first place. Why? Because consumer driven spirituality is based on the product, the spiritual teacher or the technique, and not on the gradual process that takes the whole person further along the spiritual path.

The Fourth Roadblock: The Loss of Community

In the first chapter, I shared some of my up-bringing in an Eastern European ethnic community. It was in this community, where the major institutions were church and family, that I learned about spirituality. With holiday celebrations, family gatherings, and church services, there was a blending of custom, ritual and meaning that permeated life. As my family grew and my siblings moved away from our parental home, many of these customs and rituals were lost. For me, many of them are now a formative memory of a different time.

I have several friends who are Native American. They have shared with me about their cultures, languages, and customs. These things play a different role in each of their lives. Yet, for each of them, it is clear that with the disintegration of Native American life (the result of calculated Federal policy including the forced suppression of religious practice), their cultures, languages, and spiritualities are quickly fading.

I was taught as a child that American culture was a great melting pot of differences that were blended together. In recent years, it has become politically correct to speak of America as a great tossed salad rather than a melting pot. In the tossed salad imagery, each vegetable is identifiable and maintains its own flavor. In reality, the melting pot imagery is a more accurate reflection of the growth of American society. Individual cultural differences are private, to be celebrated on holidays and special observances. But for day-to-day life, our cultural backgrounds are not relevant to the society at large.

The loss of ethnic and cultural differences is significant in regard to spiritual growth and development. That is because spiritual growth is rooted within the context of a tradition and maintained by a community of individuals walking the same spiritual path. Spirituality is a unique and personal dimension of an individual's life. But spirituality is fostered in a community. It is through long-term, on-going association with a group of people on a similar spiritual path that real growth occurs.

Why is this so? It is in the context of relationships with others over time that the shared experiences, stories, meanings, and contexts of spirituality are best transmitted.

As American society grows and changes, people move more frequently and live farther away from their family of origin, an on-going shift occurs away from community values to an increased sense of the importance of the individual. This rugged individualism places a person at odds with the community; increases personal isolation; and makes the individual's experience the most important measure of meaning, purpose, and value.

Through technological advances, values based on the importance of the individual in opposition to the community are transmitted at an alarming rate to other countries and cultures via satellite TV and the Internet. The result is the erosion of cultures on a global scale. The erosion of other cultures and communities is a movement toward one global culture where the traditional cultural differences are not valued or respected but supplanted by a dominant culture.

The transition to a global culture based on American values of individualism brings with it an increasingly mobile and self-alienated society. The role of the community is diminished and the role of the individual takes on greater importance.

The implication for spiritual growth and development is that spirituality becomes increasingly subjective and the role of a community is minimized. When the individual alone is the primary focus in spiritual growth, then the measure of spiritual growth becomes the frequency of individual spiritual experiences. A collection of individual, isolated spiritual experiences does not build the integrated spiritual life that comes from walking a spiritual path. Isolated spiritual experiences will leave a person more frustrated and self-alienated than never having explored spirituality in the first place.

Walking a spiritual path is making the spiritual journey with others. Those others along the path include those of former generations who walked the same path and have handed down the wisdom of their journey;

those who walk with us in the present and provide support and encouragement; and those of future generations who will follow in our steps, those to whom we hand on a spiritual tradition. This community provides both context and meaning for our spiritual journey and prevents subjective self-absorption where the measure of spiritual growth becomes the experience of a spiritual high.

Part Two

Accounts of Travelers Making the Journey

Chapter 6

Darlene Begins the Spiritual Journey

Beginning to develop the spiritual dimension of life is often confusing for people. That's especially true for adults who are accomplished in many other areas of their lives. Many people have a sense that something is missing in life. What is it? How do you figure it out? If it's spiritual, what is spirituality? How do I get it?

Those were the kind of questions Darlene asked herself. This thing called, "spirituality" was very confusing for her. She thought it was something that people in 12-step programs or abused women talked about in order to cope with their troubles. But her life was great. She was approaching fifty and in the middle of a successful corporate career. The only part of her life that really hadn't gone as planned was her divorce. There were a couple of tough years after she found out that her husband was having an affair with another woman. The differences between Darlene and her husband became irreconcilable. They divorced. She ended up with the two kids and the house. After a few years, he stopped paying child support. Darlene's response was to work it out herself. She prided herself on being strong. She pushed harder at work and got the promotions she sought. She got to the point where she was making twice as much money as her ex-husband. In the end, she was able to pay for her kids' education at very good schools, while continuing to work with an eye on a vice-presidency in her corporation.

Once her kids had finished college and were beginning their own careers, she noticed something about her own life. She jokingly referred to it as, "the empty-nest syndrome." She told her friends that it finally hit. She said that she felt funny with the kids being on their own. The truth was, she felt very alone.

It wasn't that Darlene didn't have friends. Darlene was involved in her neighborhood association, had friends she played tennis with, and was involved with Sam. Sam was a male friend who was also divorced. They dated for about six years but really weren't interested in marriage. They enjoyed each other's companionship, went to parties and other social events together, and sometimes vacationed together. While Sam spent occasional weekends at Darlene's home, they mostly led separate lives.

As time passed, Darlene had more and more sleepless nights. She was feeling a bit sad. She tried to focus more on her work and took on more responsibilities. Yet, she was aware of feeling alone. It often struck her when she'd fly to other cities for work. On the plane, she had time to think.

Darlene wondered if what she was feeling was something that was related to menopause. She went to her doctor who spoke with her after a complete examination. As they talked, the doctor told her that she was quite healthy physically. The doctor thought that Darlene was mildly depressed and wrote her a prescription for a commonly used anti-depressant. The doctor assured Darlene that the medication would help her feel better in a couple of weeks. But if she didn't feel better, she was told to just come back.

The anti-depressant did help Darlene sleep and generally feel better. Yet, she still felt alone in the world, wondering what her life meant.

Shortly after starting the anti-depressant, Darlene received an unexpected award at work for outstanding performance. Both colleagues and friends congratulated her. Talking with the company president, who patted her on the back, Darlene was told that if she kept up the good work it wouldn't be long before they'd have to move her office and change her name plate, indicating the promotion to vice-president was indeed on the horizon. As part of the award, Darlene was given a week's vacation for two at an island resort. She and Sam would take the week to relax, have fun, and enjoy tropical life.

Everything was perfect on the vacation: the resort, the island, and the companionship. Yet, Darlene wasn't into it. She couldn't enjoy the time or the honor of the award. That puzzled her a great deal. "After all," she wondered, "isn't this what I always wanted? Isn't this what's supposed to make me happy?" Darlene wasn't happy at all.

After the trip, one of Darlene's friends, realizing that Darlene wasn't herself, invited her to attend church one Sunday. Darlene was never much of a church go-er. Her family attended church when she was small, but since her teenage years, Darlene was never involved in religious activities. Usually at Christmas, sometimes on Easter, she would take her children to an Episcopal Church. She wanted her children to be exposed to the church and its customs, but didn't want to be more involved than that.

Reluctantly, Darlene accepted the invitation to go with her friend to church that Sunday. She knew that her friend was very happy and enthusiastic about the church. "Perhaps this kind of connection is what I'm missing," Darlene thought to herself.

The church they attended was a contemporary Protestant congregation. Darlene was fascinated by how well orchestrated everything was. The music was well performed. An acting troupe retold a story from the Bible. The minister, dressed in a sport shirt and jacket, gave an impressive delivery accented with jokes and stories, while walking freely in the aisles. It wasn't anything like what Darlene had expected.

Over brunch, her friend asked Darlene what she thought. Darlene said it was more fun and entertaining than she expected and that she was impressed with how professionally it was all done. Her friend smiled. Darlene asked what her friend got out of being involved in the church.

The friend shared that the church gave her a sense of belonging somewhere to a group of people who cared and shared similar values. The sermons gave her perspective on life and the services themselves were always a positive lift. "I always leave feeling good," Darlene's friend told her.

Darlene attended the church a few more times, but each time she went she became more aware at how highly controlled the experience was. She realized that the church used many of the same techniques used by corporations for marketing and training. That disappointed her because Darlene suspected that church was probably just as much about public relations, marketing, and putting the right "spin" on things as corporate life. She wasn't going to be taken in by an emotionally based marketing pitch when what she wanted was something substantive for her life.

At the same time, the experience at church made Darlene think that perhaps it was spirituality she was seeking. She went to a bookstore and looked through several books. Sitting in the bookstore, drinking cappuccino, paging through the books she selected, Darlene ran into another friend. Darlene was a bit embarrassed as her friend examined the books. Her friend smiled. "I'd recommend this one. And this one, well, I just don't get into spirits and angels." Darlene asked her friend, "How do you know about this stuff?" Her friend shared with her about a women's spirituality group she attended. "It's not about religion or church. We each believe what we want to. It's about finding yourself and getting spiritually in touch with Mother Earth." Darlene found this interesting. It was something she wasn't familiar with. She bought the book her friend recommended and agreed to go to a meeting of the group.

At the meeting, Darlene found a group of about twenty women. Most of the women appeared to be over 35, with some perhaps in their sixties or seventies. The women were discussing an article they had read in preparation for the meeting. Darlene heard the women talking about "women's issues" and "a feminist perspective." She wondered if she hadn't walked into a meeting of political feminists and thought about leaving. Then one of the women Darlene suspected was older than she began talking about the changes that occurred in her life after her children left home. She heard the woman talk about the same kind of loneliness she experienced. The woman said that she realized that she never took time to develop her spirituality. She came to see that when the children were on their own. This woman shared that the time she now had was really an opportunity. She started writing poetry and learned to paint. The woman said that now that she's retired, it's her spiritual connection that's the most important thing to her.

Some women spoke echoing this theme. Others talked about things that sounded odd to Darlene. One woman, who wore a pastel gauze dress and several sets of beads, talked about feeling her womanpower when she drummed. Darlene could only think of her oldest son playing drums in the family room as a teenager. Another woman talked about the spiritual experience she had at a pow wow and wanting to learn more from Native Americans. The only experience Darlene had of anything Indian was visiting a casino. The women who interested Darlene most were the ones who talked about feeling a connection with the things around them in their every day lives. One woman talked about running in a park near her home and the experience of feeling set free. She would begin the run by taking time to sit under a favorite tree and let herself get quiet. She described the run as helping her to set an internal rhythm.

Darlene didn't say much during that meeting. She mostly listened and realized that other women were looking for the same things she was. It appeared that several of the women had found the missing piece in their lives. That encouraged her to come back for more meetings.

In time, Darlene had the courage to say that she really didn't understand spirituality. She said that she thought it was something she needed in her life but didn't know where to begin. The group focused its attention on Darlene and encouraged her to tell her story. While it felt strange to talk about personal things to strangers, Darlene talked about her family, career, and relationship with Sam. She said that she was discouraged because it seemed like everything was good in her life. Yet, she had feelings of emptiness and of being alone in the world. Some women responded with how they'd experienced similar things in their lives. The words that touched her most were from the older woman Darlene listened to in the first meeting. She told Darlene that it took her several years to find herself. But that after taking time to slow down and pay attention to her life, she began to understand what spirituality meant. She read books like Anne Morrow Lindbergh's **Gift of the Sea** and Anne Dillard's **Pilgrim at Tinker Creek**. Based on those books, she paid more attention to the rhythms of nature and took time for herself. That was how she came to develop the spiritual dimension of her life.

After the meeting, Darlene arranged to meet the woman for coffee later in the week. As they talked, Darlene found that she and this woman, Jan, had many things in common. After her children had grown and were independent, Jan felt something was missing in her life. While she was married, her husband had his work and golf buddies. The children moving on didn't seem to affect him in the same way that it did her. Jan tried volunteering and becoming involved in community groups. While that helped fill the time, it didn't address the deeper feelings she had. She had been drawn to nature and began reading books by women about nature. The books that struck her had a contemplative dimension, like the ones she recommended to Darlene during the meeting. That led her to paint and write poetry as well as to take time to reflect and meditate.

"I have a little garden in my back yard," Jan told Darlene. "I often sit in the garden and just let my mind get quiet. Once I feel quiet inside, I look at the flowers or birds and just watch what they do. I don't know if it's really meditation, but that's what I call it. It helps me to stay balanced and keep things in perspective."

Jan's husband had died a few years earlier. Jan said that while it was difficult to lose him after the 41 years of marriage, having time in her special place to reflect and meditate helped her to get through the loss. "I sometimes still talk to him," Jan said. "When I need to, I go to the garden and talk. I know he's there. He knew it was a special place for me."

Jan suggested that Darlene find a place for herself and spend time there as often as possible. "Don't do anything. Just go and sit there till you're really quiet inside. I think it helps to do it in the same place. I get too distracted if I don't go to the same place. Getting quiet inside really helps you to see things differently. When I'm quiet inside, I can pay attention to what's really important in my life."

Jan and Darlene agreed to meet again in a few weeks. As Darlene was leaving, she felt really good about the conversation she had with Jan. She felt as if someone understood what she was experiencing. She also thought, "Sitting and being quiet? It sounds so simple. Will it really do anything?"

Darlene walked in a park near her home a few times each week. There were benches there, but she never took time to sit down and stay in the park. There was always something to get back home to do. The day after she met with Jan, she decided that she would take 15 minutes after her walk and just sit on a bench. Walking usually helped her sort things in her mind. She thought that it might be good to just take the time to be quiet once she had her walk.

While walking, she checked out where each bench was located. She wanted to pick one in a secluded place, but in a place she thought looked appealing. As she made her laps around the park, one bench in particular looked good to her. When she finished the walk, she went over to it and looked closely at the setting. Deciding that it was the right spot, she sat down. Darlene was very serious about this and wanted to be sure to do things just right. She sat up straight with her hands on her lap, took a deep breath, and closed her eyes. With her eyes closed, it seemed as if things were getting darker and darker. She said to herself, "I want to do this right. I want to let everything to get quiet inside. I want this to work for me." After a few minutes which seemed much longer than that to her, Darlene felt very still inside. The only thing she was aware of was her breathing. She slowly opened her eyes. She was surprised because everything seemed much brighter, more colorful, sharper, and crisper. Under a tree near her, a squirrel was sitting very still. She watched the squirrel as it picked up something, looked at it in between chewing it, then darted a few feet away, and was still again. Something about watching the squirrel captivated her. She was amazed at how alert it was, and how focused. Yet, it seemed very calm while it didn't miss anything around it. Darlene thought, "Well, maybe I do need to be more like a squirrel: alert, focused, while remaining at peace." Just as she was thinking that, someone came walking near the squirrel and it ran up the backside of the tree. Darlene laughed thinking, "Today's lesson on being a squirrel must be done." She looked at her watch as she stood up. She realized that 25 minutes had passed. To her, it seemed like she was only watching the squirrel for a very short time while she had been on the bench almost half an hour.

Darlene returned to that bench several times a week. While traveling for work, she missed that time. She knew she needed to find ways to do similar things while on the road.

With Jan's encouragement, Darlene began to incorporate time to be quiet with her activities each day. While her busy schedule made this difficult for her, she learned to schedule it on her calendar as she did her other appointments. Darlene prided herself on doing what was scheduled. She figured that if it was in her appointment book, she would be sure to have her quiet time.

Darlene found that the quiet time each day helped to keep her from being over-stressed with other things. She started to see people differently. It became clear to her how most people were stressed, over-worked, and on-the-edge in one way or another. The quiet time helped Darlene pace herself. She was more focused in working and better able to step back from the work when it was time for it to be done.

Some days, the quiet time provided her with insight. Most days, it was simply a routine. Whether the time provided special insights or not, Darlene saw the changes regular quiet time made in her life. Over a period of several months, she realized that when she did not make space for quiet time on a regular basis, her life went back to the way it was before: hectic and stressful. That made her more avid about taking the time she needed.

Reading, meeting occasionally with Jan, attending the meetings of the women's group, and having time for inner quiet had all been positive steps for Darlene. About a year after she first attended the women's group, she was again looking for something more. She knew that spirituality was an important part of her life. Now she wanted to expand her understanding of it.

Much to her surprise, Darlene found her opportunity to learn more while flying across country on a business trip. Paging through the airline magazine found in the seat pocket, Darlene saw an ad for a women's spirituality event. The event was a several day wilderness experience that included lodging in cabins in a remote location as well as white water rafting and mountain hiking. Each day there were conferences on meditation using both breathing techniques and movement. To make the event complete, there were a massage therapist and a spa on-site. A gourmet chef prepared meals. It sounded perfect to Darlene.

Later that day, she called to request information about the women's spirituality wilderness experience. She shared the information with Jan and other women from the spirituality group. They joked about the massage therapist and gourmet chef. Through the jokes, Darlene decided that this was the kind of experience she needed.

Attending the five-day experience proved very beneficial to Darlene. It put her in a totally different environment so that she could be away from her day-to-day routine. It gave her the relaxation and pampering she needed away from work. The experience also provided time to exercise and use her body in ways she missed. Most of all, through the seminars and workshops she took the next step in her spiritual development.

The instructors affirmed the progress she had made on her own in meditation. Based on her experience, they taught her methods of meditation like focusing on her breath as well as exercises using her imagination.

Darlene also learned about keeping a journal of her experiences. In time, she would find the journal a very useful tool for her.

Darlene returned refreshed and invigorated, having taken care of herself by really getting away and by learning new, practical things to incorporate in her spiritual life. She realized that sometime during the past year, sometime after she started making quiet time part of each day, that the feelings of being sad and alone in the world were gone. Now, she felt connected. Connected to what? She wasn't sure. But she felt a part of some larger whole in nature or the universe. She still didn't have words for it. Whatever it was, she was glad for it.

At a time in Darlene's life when she felt alone, isolated, and incomplete, she had the courage to seek answers that made sense to her. She wasn't willing to accept easy solutions but continued to look and explore until she found what was right for her. The solution was so simple it must have seemed a bit humorous to her. Darlene found what she needed in her life by simply taking time to quiet her mind and be present to herself and life as it was around her. As she learned to be content to simply be silent, she was able to let go of the other distractions in her life that prevented her from living a spiritually focused life. Finding others to talk to about spirituality was very helpful. It was through the encouragement of the women's group, and particularly from Jan, that Darlene took the initial steps to begin her spiritual journey.

While it's true that most people can't afford a weeklong wilderness experience with a gourmet chef and massage therapist, it is also true that the important lessons Darlene learned were quite simple. In a few workshops she learned how to take the next few steps along her spiritual journey. These steps including learning a little more about meditation techniques and about journaling.

Starting the journey along a spiritual path is really quite simple, as Darlene learned in time. Perhaps it is so simple that many people simply miss it.

Chapter 7
Dwayne: Re-Discovering Self on the Good Road

Dwayne's a likeable guy. He's the kind of guy everyone enjoys being around. He's friendly, out-going and personable. He's someone you can depend on.

At age 31, Dwayne has had what he's considered a pretty good life. After four years in the Air Force, he returned to civilian life. With Air Force training in computer systems, he found a job in a high-tech firm. It wasn't long before he met a woman he liked. By age 25, Dwayne was married with the first child on the way.

Dwayne continued to enjoy going out with the guys on the weekends. Sometimes, his wife would accompany him. He liked to play pool, watch sports on TV, and play his music. Dwayne played guitar and enjoyed performing. A local bar hired him to play Saturday nights. Dwayne thought that was a good thing because he could make money doing what he enjoyed. His wife, however, saw it differently.

Dwayne often worked late during the week. When he also started playing Saturday at the bar, Dwayne's wife felt that they had no time together.

When tension arose over the Saturday night job, Dwayne realized that there were problems in his marriage.

From Dwayne's perspective, he was doing everything he could. He worked hard, provided the best home he could, and found a way to bring in some extra money to provide more for his family. He loved his wife. He also enjoyed spending time with the guys. Spending time with the guys and working Saturday nights didn't mean he loved her less. He didn't understand what the problem was, but it was clear to him that there was a problem.

Dwayne's wife, Sandi, felt trapped with managing the house and caring for their son. She felt that she was doing it alone. She worked part-time, but her work did little more than pay for childcare. At her insistence, they saw a marriage counselor.

From Dwayne's perspective, counseling made things worse. He found out more things that were wrong than he had realized previously. He really didn't blame the counselor. But Dwayne was feeling overwhelmed. He realized that his wife was very unhappy in the marriage. He felt blamed, but didn't know what to do about it.

Dwayne remembered how much his wife enjoyed their dating and engagement. He tried to be more romantic. A couple of times, he arranged to have friends baby-sit so that he and his wife could go out for a romantic dinner and dancing. He tried to be more passionate. That resulted in a second pregnancy for his wife. This confused Dwayne as he thought Sandi was taking birth control pills. While he was surprised by the pregnancy because he thought they decided that this wasn't the time for a second child, Dwayne took pride in being a good father and was supportive of his wife. In time, Sandi admitted during a counseling session that when Dwayne was more amorous, she stopped taking birth control pills. She thought that having another child would keep Dwayne home evenings and weekends.

Dwayne tried to explain that the evenings he wasn't home he was at work. While he enjoyed the Saturday night job playing, it was still work.

He made good tips and the money was very helpful. His only social time with the guys was one or two Sunday afternoons a month to watch a game on TV. Otherwise, he was working.

The counselor talked with them about communication and learning to work together as a couple. Dwayne didn't understand what there was to talk about. Life seemed pretty simple to him. His wife kept saying that he didn't meet her needs. But what were her needs? Dwayne pointed out that they had a good home, enough money, that he didn't drink or abuse her, and that he was affectionate. Dwayne honestly didn't know what else to do, but understood that he wasn't giving Sandi what she wanted. Sandi kept saying that Dwayne couldn't meet her needs. But Dwayne didn't understand what these unmet needs were.

Time passed slowly. The second child, a girl, was born. About a year after the birth of their second child, Sandi filed for a divorce.

In the divorce settlement, Sandi and the children kept the house. Dwayne paid over half of his income in alimony and child support. He was crushed. He left the marriage not understanding what went wrong. He thought of himself as a good provider. It remained confusing to him.

After Dwayne was settled in his new apartment and adjusted to life as a single man, he began to think more about his future. He knew that he had progressed as far as he could at work. He needed a degree for advancement.

Dwayne checked out several programs and decided on a university with programs designed for working adults. He enrolled and began to take classes one night a week. It was at the university that I met Dwayne.

Dwayne was one of my students in an undergraduate psychology class. It was an elective for his information systems program. Dwayne was one of the best students in the class. He was always prepared for class, had relevant comments to make during discussions, and wrote interesting papers.

During break, Dwayne and I talked occasionally in a lounge down the hall from the classroom. He'd speak fondly of his children, how much he enjoyed his work, and his plans for grad school. Given our break time conversations, it came as a surprise to me to learn that Dwayne was divorced. That came out during a class discussion on stress management. As we talked about life stresses in class, Dwayne shared that the divorce was the most stressful event in his life.

On the last night of class, as I was walking to my car, Dwayne stopped me to talk. He said that he enjoyed the class and found the discussions with me thoughtful. He expressed his disappointment that it was over. After telling Dwayne that I also enjoyed his contributions to the class, I suggest that he call if he wanted to talk or go out for coffee.

A few weeks passed and the class faded in my memory as I moved on to different projects. To my surprise, Dwayne did call. We met at a local eatery with patio dining. We took time to talk more about our pasts. Dwayne wasn't aware that I was a minister and worked in the area of spiritual development. Knowing that I was a psychologist, he assumed that was my only career endeavor.

Dwayne looked at me in a thoughtful way. "I don't mean to offend you," he started, "but you seem too normal to be a priest." I laughed and retorted, "Who said I was normal?" "What I mean is that you seem to have a handle on real life," Dwayne replied. Then he asked, "What's it like to be a priest?"

I took a deep breath and thought about how to answer Dwayne's question. "First, I'm a Protestant minister, so that's a little bit different than being a priest, but it's basically the same field," I explained. "I'm not serving a church right now, but I have. Like anyone else, I still have bills to pay, groceries to buy, and all the other details of life to take care of." Dwayne had an astonished look on his face. "You were the priest in a church?" he asked. "Yeah, actually, I started a church and was the pastor for a few years when I lived in Miami. But I don't think that's the important part about why I'm a minister." Dwayne started to listen more carefully. "The truth is that my spiritual life is very important to me. It's the most important aspect of my life. It's so important to me that I want to help others find a way to walk a spiritual path that's right

Accounts of Travelers Making the Journey   75

for them. Most of the work I do in counseling is related to spirituality and the things that prevent people from walking a spiritual path." Dwayne asked me to explain what I meant.

I went on to tell Dwayne that I thought most people in our culture lived such busy lives with so much pressure that they lose their hearts, their spirits. Life becomes a matter of meeting goals and deadlines. One day, most people wake up and realize that they've just been running on a treadmill, putting out lots of effort, but not really getting anywhere.

As I paused to check to be sure that I was communicating clearly, Dwayne looked down at the table. I slowly began to speak. "That's how I feel most of the time. Between work, and school, and trying to be there for my kids, well, I'm just not sure who I am. The only time I feel right inside is playing my music."

I asked Dwayne to tell me about his music. I learned that he had been playing guitar since he was 9 or 10. Not only did he perform on Saturdays, playing popular music, but also he used to write songs. As he talked about writing music, his face began to glow. There was both peace and excitement about what he was saying. "When was the last time you wrote something?" I asked. He shrugged his shoulders. "It's been years, I guess," Dwayne said, as his head sank down again and he gazed into the table.

I thought for a few moments and then asked, "Can we get together sometime so that I can hear you play. I'd really like to hear your music." Dwayne looked embarrassed. He said that it really wasn't that good. I told him that I wasn't giving out Grammy Awards. I was just interested in my friend's work and what made him happy. Dwayne smiled. Before we left that evening, we set up a time to get together so that I could hear Dwayne play his own music.

A couple of weeks later, on a Saturday afternoon, I went to Dwayne's apartment. It was much like you'd expect from a divorced man's apartment: small, not well furnished, and a bit disorganized. Dwayne cleared a place on the sofa for me to sit and offered me a beer. Then he paused and asked; "Do priests drink?" I shot him a look over the top of my eyeglasses. "Just get me a beer," I said.

Over the next few hours, I sat and listened as Dwayne talked about his music, what was happening in his life, and played and sang. His music was filled with deep, personal emotion. It was clear that he worked through times of pain and confusion as well as dreams and joys through his music.

"Why don't you write more?" I asked. "I'm busy. It's just hard to find the time," Dwayne answered. I asked Dwayne first how he felt singing his music and later what it was like to write it. He answered both questions much the same way. He told me that when he wrote and when he sang, it was like something inside of him was connected. He didn't know what it was. But he said that something inside felt right. Dwayne explained that it wasn't that the music made him feel good. Some of the songs were filled with hurt, remorse, and sadness. But with those songs, as he said, "Something is workin' for me. It's just right."

I talked with Dwayne about spirituality. I explained that I understood spirituality as a dimension to human experience that provided us with meaning, purpose, and value in our life. I told him that from my perspective, spirituality enables us to make a connection between ourselves and something beyond us. From that perspective, I told Dwayne that I see his music as being very spiritual. He nervously laughed and shook his head. I continued. "Dwayne, when you're writing or singing, you told me that something felt 'right' inside of you. I think that's because you're moving beyond your emotions and making some meaningful connection through the music. When you sang a song about moving out from your family and leaving your kids, it wasn't just that you missed your kids and felt sad. There was a depth of meaning in that song that made it real and it came alive." Dwayne slowly nodded in agreement. "Through your music, you're finding a kind of meaning or purpose to your experience. Your experience takes on a different value. It's real and alive."

Dwayne and I talked more about that as he tried to understand his music from a broader perspective.

I told him that I thought it would be good to approach both singing and writing as a spiritual practice. Maybe once a week, he could plan time to write. Then another time, perhaps one evening a week, just take an hour to sing some of his stuff. I suggested that he keep a journal of what happens, to just conclude the time by writing for five minutes about what happened during that time.

Dwayne took my advice seriously and made a routine of playing and writing for himself. Over the next several months, when we would get together, Dwayne would tell me about the music that he was writing as well as the thoughts and emotions he wrote out. Over time, Dwayne was becoming more expressive. At first I thought it was just that we were getting more comfortable with each other. Then I realized that he was learning to express his feelings more and more.

One evening we met for dinner. While eating burritos at a little Mexican place, Dwayne told me that he had written a few songs about his divorce. He said that it was difficult for him to put his feelings about the divorce into words. Staring at his food as he talked, he said that he cried a lot about it. "I'd never admit that to anyone else," he said. I smiled and said, "Yeah, I know. It's a guy thing." That brought a smirk to his face as he continued. "Writing the music, singing it, and then keeping that journal helped me realize something," Dwayne said very carefully. "I understand now that my wife wanted me to communicate my feelings and I didn't know how. I'm still not sure I know how. I did the things for her that I knew were right. I just couldn't talk about it."

I asked Dwayne to consider that he's always had a way to communicate his feelings. He did that through his music. The problem was he had stopped using the way that worked for him, or at least he didn't use it with his wife when they were married. I suggested that he's developed at least two more ways in recent months to express his feelings: writing the journal and talking. After all, he was talking to me about his feelings. He even admitted that he cried. I pointed out that if he could do it with me, he could learn to do it with someone else, too. "I never thought of it that way, " Dwayne responded, "But it does make lots of sense."

Dwayne continued to use his music to sort through his feelings. His ability to express his emotions and thoughts grew a great deal. In time, he started using some simple techniques for meditation and explored more of his inner life.

I don't see Dwayne very often. I do know that while Sandi dated a few men, she never became seriously involved. Dwayne called once and asked if I could recommend a good therapist for them to see. While I suspected he wanted to make an appointment with me, I referred him to a colleague who specializes in work with couples. I suggested that they focus on their communication as a couple and see where that leads them. I suspect that there's a good chance that Dwayne and Sandi may get back together. But even if they don't, after a few sessions of counseling Dwayne will have a better understanding of what's not working in that relationship.

As for his journey on a spiritual path, Dwayne needed to begin walking the good road by finding healing for parts of himself that he previously avoided. Many men never develop the skills to pay attention to and properly express their emotions. Over time, they get used to life without this major part of themselves. Walking the good road often includes reclaiming parts of ourselves we've lost along the way. As Dwayne rediscovered himself through his music, he was ready to go further on his journey along the spiritual path.

Chapter 8

Tony: The Process of Inner Healing

Over the years, I've led many workshops and classes on spiritual themes. One class I particularly enjoy teaching is centering prayer. You may recall from chapter 3 that centering prayer is a simple method of meditation. When teaching it to a group, as in a workshop or class, I have the opportunity to provide people with a simple, easy to use technique that can radically change their spiritual lives. It's exciting for me to introduce people to this form of prayer.

It was during a class on centering prayer and spirituality that I met Tony. The class lasted a couple of hours one evening a week for six weeks. A group of about a dozen people was in the class. Tony was the most eager participant.

Tony was a warm, welcoming guy with a great sense of humor. He was a musician. He played piano with a local symphony and organ as a church musician.

Over the years, Tony worked in a variety of different Christian churches, mostly Roman Catholic, Episcopal, Methodist, and Congregational. He also filled in at synagogues every now and then. I remember someone asking Tony about his denominational affiliation. He smiled and retorted, "I keep it simple: whoever is paying me that week is whose church I belong to. Sometimes I'm Jewish on Friday and find Jesus again by Sunday." Tony usually responded to personal questions with quick humor that made others smile, but also kept him from revealing a great deal about himself.

In the class, Tony was the first to arrive and the last to leave. As part of the closing prayer each week, I'd teach simple chants to use for prayer. Tony offered to teach the group how to properly sing Gregorian chant. I thanked him with a smile, and reminded him that this wasn't a performance group. "I'm not worried about quality singing," I told Tony. "Open hearts for prayer is what we need here." Not wanting to be out-done, Tony quickly came back with, "Well, don't come to the church I'm playing at now. The choir is getting ready to record a CD but I'm sure no one in that church prays, unless it's for a short sermon or a good parking space." Tony's humor was always quick-witted and sometimes had a jagged edge.

As the class began using the techniques of centering prayer, Tony was quick to grasp the method. From the first time we used centering prayer in class, Tony shared his excitement. He found it peaceful, quieting, and refreshing. He said it made him feel almost instantly in tune with himself. When others in the class struggled with intrusive thoughts or simply felt nothing at all, Tony encouraged them. I remember him saying to a few people, "Just keep doing it. It's really great. You'll see."

Then, one week, the change occurred. I arrived to set-up for the class and Tony was waiting for me. As I got out of my car, I could see him near the door of the church activities building where the class was held. He looked very serious, and a little worn out.

"I need to talk to you, Rev," were Tony's first words to me. I asked what was happening. Tony continued, "I don't know what happened. But something's wrong with this centering prayer stuff." I inquired, "What do you mean?" "I guess I'm doing something wrong cause it doesn't feel good anymore. Actually, every time I do it now, it just hurts. I'm having trouble sleeping, too. It seems like I can't relax." I reminded

Tony that this is one of the things that sometimes happen for people when using any form of meditation properly. I offered to schedule time to talk with him privately, but asked that he consider sharing what was happening for him with the other members of the class. "Some of it's sort of personal," Tony said cautiously. "You don't need to share anything you don't want others to know. That's up to you. I do think it will help others if you tell them what's happening. You don't need to tell the class about any memories or dreams you're having. Sharing the feelings you encounter will probably help you and the others." He said he'd think about it, as he helped me set up the classroom. It wasn't long before others from the class arrived.

In the class, Tony shared briefly about his experience. He said that over the last week, when he would begin a time of centering prayer, he found that he initially quieted down inside. Out of the inner quiet, he'd start to feel a little bit anxious followed by a pervasive sense of pain. He would hurt inside. He talked about trying to stop the pain and quitting the period of prayer before he completed the amount of time he intended to pray. Another person in the group said that happened to her. "I returned to repeating the prayer word on my breath because I was aware of the pain. It hurt so much that I couldn't avoid it. But using the prayer word, the pain passed and I felt something in me let go," she explained. Tony admitted that he hadn't done that. He just wanted rid of it. "You just got to go with it, whether you like it or not," another class member commented. "I'm starting to learn that the important thing is doing it, not what it feels like." I affirmed that using the method of prayer regularly was indeed the important aspect. Some times will feel great; others will be filled with distractions; some will hurt; still others will feel like nothing much is happening at all. That's all part of the process.

I used this conversation as part of the class's instruction that night. I reminded the group that when we experience pain in meditation, it's usually because we've repressed something in our past. The pain is a sign that something needs to be healed. The pain is the reminder that something is wounded and needs to be healed by the light of day. Sometimes we'll know what it is. Sometimes it passes without being clearly identified.

Inner pain, psychic pain, spiritual pain are all like physical pain. I remember as a young child being taken to the doctor's office and getting an injection. My parents tried to explain many times that I shouldn't look at the needle and just relax so that it wouldn't hurt. What did I do when I was three and four years old? Of course, I looked at the needle as it was coming, clenched my arm tight, and screamed at the top of my lungs. Eventually, I learned to take a deep breath, relax, and then the prick of the needle passed quickly and relatively easily. No matter what the pain, whether painful emotions or the pain of childbirth, the pain passes more easily when we move with it rather than fight against it.

The class talked about the importance of using a journal to record these experiences as well as to move through the feelings by writing them out. The process of putting our feelings on paper often helps to get them out so that we aren't holding onto them. A couple of people in the class also shared how this helped them with their process of centering prayer. Tony smiled and said, "Okay. I'm stopping at a store on the way home to get a new notebook for a journal. On second thought, the way I've been feeling, I'll get two notebooks." The group chuckled as I wondered what was really happening inside Tony.

A few days later, Tony came to my office. Because I didn't know much about Tony, I asked about him, his family, and his life in general. Tony, in his early forties, was a gay man from a large Italian family. He grew up in a Philadelphia Italian neighborhood where many of the ethnic traditions included church. The only thing he particularly liked about church was the music. Because he could use the church organ to practice, he started to play for services at a neighborhood church when he was a teenager.

Tony's family didn't have a great deal of difficulty with his being gay. He came out to them after he finished college. He looked back and realized that they probably knew about his sexual orientation all along. While his brothers played stickball in the streets in the evening, he studied music and practiced at church. In his youth, he didn't have a lot of friends his own age. He gravitated to adults who encouraged his artistic interests. He also took voice lessons. As a teenager, while his peers bought contemporary music at the record store, he was in the library listening to opera. He claimed that his mother's disappointment with him was that he didn't become a priest. She assumed that if he was in church, it was for religious reasons. For Tony, it was the music and the pipe organ.

There were times when Tony was teased by other kids in school and in the neighborhood for being gay. Mostly, though, Tony was a loner. In college, he began to develop his sense of humor. He felt it put people at ease. I remember his adding, "Everyone likes a funny guy."

After college, Tony found decent jobs using his musical talents. He was talented enough to tour a few European countries. But Tony wasn't the caliber of musician he dreamed of becoming. While he made a much better living in music than most people, he wouldn't be the performer he hoped to be.

What I heard Tony describe was a lonely childhood and a sense of dissatisfaction with how his life turned out. It was not surprising that Tony turned to alcohol in his twenties to ease the ache he felt inside. He became a solitary alcoholic, often going home at night to drink himself to sleep.

Tony was an attractive man. He admitted it was usually easy to find sexual partners. When he was younger, he took advantage of that to find companionship for the night. Rarely did he allow men to become part of his life for more than a few nights. Except for Kevin.

Kevin was Tony's only real love. Kevin was seven years younger than Tony. They met at a party after a concert Tony played. Kevin introduced himself to Tony and came on strong. It was a whirlwind romance where Kevin swept Tony off his feet.

That was in the late 1980's. Tony and Kevin were together for little more than two years. The relationships simply couldn't last. Kevin had AIDS.

Shortly after Kevin and Tony started dating, Kevin spent most of his time at Tony's home. From Tony's perspective, it was natural for him to move in. When Kevin became ill, there was no place for him to go. His religiously conservative family wanted nothing to do with him. He had no other close friends. Tony cared for his new, young lover through his death. After completing the funeral, Tony settled all the affairs of Kevin's estate. Kevin had died about three years before I met Tony.

I asked Tony about the support he had from others during this time. He told me that most of his friends jumped ship when faced with Kevin's illness. Two older women from the church Tony played at did bring meals and would sometimes sit with Kevin. The pastor of the church made it clear that he didn't want Tony talking about the situation at the church. Tony's friends in Alcoholics Anonymous told him that he was just being co-dependent by taking care of Kevin and that he needed to set better boundaries. Tony looked at me with a stone cold face and said, "I did this like I've done everything else in my life: alone."

The year after Kevin's death was particularly hard for Tony. He felt that he had no one to turn to during his grief. He saw a counselor who probably did what she could. But talking to a counselor once a week doesn't make up for the lack of support from friends, family, and workplace when faced with such an overwhelming loss. Tony began to drink again, but in a few months was back at AA. He seemed to receive support there to deal with his drinking, but not the other issues he faced. He took a job at another church that was more open to gay and lesbian people and had a support group for families of people with HIV/AIDS. When a year passed after Kevin's death, Tony decided that he spent enough time in grief. It was time for it to be over. After all, he reasoned to himself, he hadn't known Kevin that long. "It wasn't like he had lost a spouse of thirty years," he said to me. To get past the grief, Tony plunged into his work. He also got involved in additional music groups.

Given everything that Tony had been through, I wasn't surprised that he was experiencing a great deal of pain in meditation. The process of centering prayer opens us to the Divine Presence in us. It also opens us to all the other things we've kept hidden inside. All of his life, Tony had pushed the pain deeper and deeper inside. Through a solitary life, marked by loneliness and isolation, Tony never learned to share his pain with others or work it out for himself. Instead, he hid it and covered it over with humor. When the pain became too great, he dulled the pain by drinking and sex. Even when the pain began to surface through the use of centering prayer, Tony wanted to get away from it as quickly as possible. Now he had the choice to make: he could either continue to suppress the pain or to deal with it in a different way.

Many people learn at an early age to suppress their feelings of pain. While Tony was very thorough in his ability to do this, it's a skill that many people have. As in Tony's case, many people considered "minorities" in our society carry a great deal of hidden pain. Gay men and lesbians grow up feeling as though they don't fit in with their heterosexual peers. While they may enjoy and be successful in the same activities as others, the largely invisible difference of sexual orientation creates an inner conflict of not belonging. The inner ache of loneliness and isolation may be intensified by experiences of prejudice and discrimination. Those wounds, often begun in childhood, continue to fester into adult life and greatly impact the ability for intimate relationships.

People from racial and cultural minorities have similar yet different experiences. Growing up in a family where racial or cultural identity is usually affirmed, the children entering the larger world beyond the family may encounter discrimination or prejudice for simply being who they were created to be. Having grown used to a life where discrimination is potentially encountered, older family members often accept these experiences as a normal part of life. The child is confused by the acceptance and affirmation received at home and in the ethnic community and the simultaneous prejudice at school or in the larger community. This confusion results in splitting parts of self, especially the emotional parts of self, in order to cope with the complex dynamic of affirmation and rejection.

Often, the emotional distancing from self is internalized and becomes a regular part of the person's experience.

The irony of it all is that there is no real majority. We are actually a society of diverse minority groups. Yet, we have failed to internalize an appreciation for this diversity in both our personal and cultural values.

Those who grew up in families where addictions or mental illness were present often carry with them a hidden pain. A child with parents who are addicts or who have serious mental illness learn quickly to hold in emotions. The free expression of emotions can lead to harm when a parent has been drinking or is having some sort of psychotic episode. A child learns to stabilize its own environment by withdrawing.

In counseling, individuals who carry pain from childhood into their adult life are often taught to express their emotions and to learn ways to use their emotions as a positive resource. While therapy is able to help many people in this process, there is also a spiritual dimension to healing that is often missing.

The process of meditation, such as centering prayer, enables a person to both encounter and move past deep emotional pain. At this level of pain, there are rarely changes that need to be made in a person's life or new coping strategies to be developed. Instead, a person encounters the pain, recognizes it for what it is, and lets it go. There may be a sense of loss or grief because of the way life was limited because of the pain. On a spiritual dimension, this process is one of coming to accept what has been.

Meditation is not the only spiritual practice that enables a person to pass through such pain. Many Native American people use the sweat lodge for this purpose. Some Native peoples have a tradition of running great distances to push through the pain. There are also Eastern practices involving dance and movement that allow a person to release deep pain. For most of us, encountering the wounded heart that is deep inside will occur when we learn to quietly sit and be present to the Mystery within us. That Mystery, which is the source of life, often lives with the pain of our past hurts.

Through regular meditation, in this case centering prayer, the pain Tony had buried within himself began to be released. While he had previously tried to stop it or control it, he learned to simply be present to it. It was a brooding experience for him, not one marked by emotional outbursts or crying. He would go through periods feeling down or sullen, but he was never really overwhelmed by it. Tony took time to write about the pain he experienced. Much of what he wrote was focused on events of his life. As he wrote, he became more reconciled with the events of his past and with the people who were part of those events. I asked him to share with the class to the degree he was comfortable. What he spoke of was in general terms. Members of the class were able to affirm his experience as well as share similar kinds of experience. However, the class was only a few weeks in length. Tony's journey through the pain would take much longer than the class.

I agreed to meet with him as a spiritual director. At first, we met every two weeks. In time, we met on a monthly basis. It was clear to me that as Tony moved beyond his pain and continued using centering prayer, he became more relaxed. He also was more open to people. The bite that had often been part of his humor faded while he developed a softer way of joking with others.

Five or six months after the class ended, Tony asked what I thought of an idea he had. He felt that he had never been able to share the loss of Kevin with anyone. He didn't want to have a memorial service or anything like that. Instead, he wanted to invite members of the class to his home for coffee and desert and just tell them about the love of his life. Tony felt safe with the members of the class. Because it was with the members of the class that he began to work through his feelings, he wanted to finish the process with them. I told him it was fine with me. The last night of the class, a list of names and addresses had been shared with the group members for those who wanted to stay in contact. I suggested that he call each member and explain the purpose of the meeting.

Most of the members of the class attended Tony's gathering. At first, he attempted to defer to me to lead the group. I gently reminded him that he was the host and I was one of the guests. While he was initially uncomfortable, he slowly began by inviting the group to begin with a period of centering prayer. After about twenty minutes of silent meditation, Tony began to tell the story of his relationship with Kevin. He began by recounting how wonderful he felt having an attractive younger man pursuing him and continuing through the events surrounding Kevin's death. Just as people laughed and chuckled at some of the amusing stories from the early part of the relationship, some also cried as Tony spoke of Kevin's death. There was clear anger in the group over the friends who walked away as well as the pastor who didn't want Tony to speak of his loss at church. When Tony finished, I asked him why he wanted to tell us about this part of his life. He looked at each member of the group and explained that it was because of the class's encouragement that he'd been able to get past so much of the pain he held on to. Now, he wanted to share his relationship with Kevin because it had been so important to him and because he felt no one had been present when it happened. He felt that now there had been witnesses to the experience he had gone through in isolation.

Indeed, the group witnessed both the emotional and spiritual growth Tony experienced as a result of engaging in regular spiritual practices. They were witnesses to his story of passion, loss, loneliness, and deep hurt. As we witnessed Tony passing through this difficult part of his journey, it was clear that he had passed through the pain and was encountering new life.

I worked with Tony for some time after this. He continued developing the spiritual dimension of his life with the simple techniques of centering prayer and journaling. In that process, he became more aware of himself, of the Divine Presence within him, and he developed greater capacity to open his heart in healthy ways to others. The lessons Tony learned were important ones. I was glad to be part of his journey.

Accounts of Travelers Making the Journey

Sometime later, included with a card, Tony sent a copy of a poem that summarized for him the process of his growth. The poem is by Wendell Berry.

> Within the circles of our lives
> we dance the circles of the years,
> the circles of the seasons
> within the circles of the years,
> the cycles of the moon
> within the circles of the seasons,
> the circles of our reasons
> within the cycles of the moon.
>
> Again, again we come and go,
> changed, changing. Hands
> join, unjoin in love and fear,
> grief and joy. The circles turn,
> each giving into each, into all.
> Only music keeps us here,
>
> each by all the others held.
> In the hold of hands and eyes
> we turn in pairs, that joining
> joining each to all again.
>
> And then we turn aside, alone,
> out of the sunlight gone
>
> into the darker circles return.

Chapter 9

The Story of Marilyn: Further Along on the Journey

Part of my own spiritual practice includes a trip each morning to the Monastery of the Benedictine Sisters of Perpetual Adoration in Tucson. I join the Benedictines and a handful of other people for morning prayer. The morning prayer service, also known by its Latin name, Lauds, is a prayer for praise for the new day. In this prayer, we chant psalms, listen to a reading from the Christian scriptures, quietly reflect and meditate, and share prayers of petition. In the monastic tradition, Lauds, and the evening service, Vespers, prayerfully attune a person to the cycle of night becoming day and day becoming night. In this way, the course of the day is punctuated with time for prayer and reflection.

One Spring, a woman began to attend morning prayer. As with most new-comers, it took her awhile to get used to the service with the chanting and prolonged periods of silence. A few times I assisted her with the prayer book so that she could follow the occasional changes. That's how I met Marilyn.

Marilyn is a single woman in her late thirties. Over several weeks, we occasionally chatted as we left the monastery chapel. Finally, one morning, we agreed to have coffee. That's when I learned more about Marilyn.

She's a professor at a local college. With the school year ended, she had more time for herself. Her goal over the summer was to write a book. She found it helpful to be up early for prayer so that she could be focused for her writing. She said that was why she attended morning prayer each day.

As time progressed, I learned a bit more about Marilyn. She was living with a man and was confused about the relationship. She wondered if her confusion about the relationship, and a series of failed past relationships, was some indicator that she should join a monastery and lead a celibate life. While several nuns she knew impressed her, some of her friends were very discouraging of her interest in monastic life. They believed that nuns were emotionally immature and unable to deal with the realities of life.

As I got to know Marilyn, I told her that I was a psychologist, a minister, and also worked with people as a spiritual director. One morning, after prayer, she asked if I would work with her. She said that she was unsure if she needed a therapist or a spiritual director, but thought she may need both.

I agreed to set up a time with her to talk about it. Making no promises, I told her that I had some concerns working as a therapist with her because we knew each other from the monastery and had shared some personal things about ourselves. I told her that one thing I wanted to do in that first meeting was talk about my concerns.

Later that week, we met at my office for an evening appointment. Marilyn told me more about herself. She had previously been married but the marriage did not work out. Her husband was a fellow graduate student. They married while in graduate school and divorced before she finished her doctoral studies. Marilyn told me that she initially found him interesting and engaging. After they were married, she felt that she was losing herself because he was emotionally strong and overpowering.

Speaking of other relationships with men, I sensed a similar pattern emerging. The man she presently lived with was a well-published scholar and academic. He was spending most of the summer lecturing at a prestigious university. Marilyn reported that no matter what her accomplishments were, and from my perspective there were several, she felt as though her boyfriend belittled them.

I asked her to describe her spiritual life. While she was Catholic, she found herself disagreeing with the Catholic Church. She saw no sound reason to prevent women from being ordained, for priests to marry, and for the Catholic Church to have a more understanding approach to issues of sexuality. What kept Marilyn attending the Catholic Church were the familiarity of the tradition and the availability of ways to nurture her spiritual life. The campus parish sponsored lectures and workshops on a regular basis that Marilyn found helpful. She also enjoyed praying at the monastery and attended Mass there during the school year. Marilyn told me a great deal about her religious practice, but it was more difficult for her to tell me about her spiritual life. So, I asked, "Who is God for you? How do you experience God's presence in your life?"

After giving my questions some thought Marilyn spoke of God in terms of a loving Father who had been present with her throughout many difficult parts of her life. She also stated feeling a certain distance from God. Because of that, based on her reading of feminist theology, she explored other images of God, including Mother, Creator, and Source of Life. Yet, these images did not convey the same depth for her as, "Father." While she spoke of God's unconditional love and presence in her life, Marilyn also spoke of wanting to please God with the decisions she made for the second half of her life. I could not help but ask if God unconditionally loved her, wasn't God already pleased with her? While she pondered that question, it didn't seem to settle easily with her.

We also discussed the possible impact our knowing each other from the monastery may have on a therapeutic relationship. We agreed that the things we discussed in our appointments would stay there and that we would be respectful of each other's privacy at the monastery and any other place we happened to meet.

Marilyn was concerned about her relationships with men and the way the relationships clouded her understanding of a possible monastic vocation. She enjoyed dating but the relationships never worked out well for her. I agreed that this would be a good thing for us to explore. I further suggested that we might choose to use hypnosis to sort out some of the relationship issues. At the same time, I stated that I would want to continue discussing her prayer life, believing that our longer-term relationship was one of spiritual direction. But I also stated that in time, it might be more appropriate for me to assist her in finding a different spiritual director.

I rarely mix my role as therapist with that of spiritual director. However, in this case I did. Marilyn seemed to have a clear understanding of the differences in the types of work these things entailed.

A therapeutic relationship with a counselor or psychologist is significantly different from working with a spiritual director. Actually, the only thing that is really common about them is both involve meeting with a person and confiding in them things not usually shared with others.

In counseling psychology, the therapeutic relationship is, in a sense, a one way street. The therapist shares little, if anything, of himself. Instead, the therapist's role is to assist a client to look at, feel, and articulate their experience of life or particular life problems. The therapist actively points out things that may be worthwhile for the client to consider, supports the client in developing strategies to resolve difficulties, and encourages the client to take the steps necessary to grow further.

The relationship with a spiritual director is significantly different from that of a therapist. The differences may be lost in the inadequate vocabulary we have for this unique relationship. In other eras, the director would have been viewed as spiritual father or mother. The role of the director is not to direct. That is, a good spiritual director does not tell someone what to do. Instead, it is understood that both people travel the journey of the spiritual life. It is presumed that the director has been walking a spiritual path for some time. What really qualifies a spiritual director to be a guide for the spiritual journey is the distance that director has covered along a spiritual path. That does not mean that the person seeking direction has nothing to teach. A spiritual director listens to, shares with, and prays with the directee. While it is understood that people make their own decisions as to how to pursue their spiritual practices, a spiritual director may openly share how the director faced similar experiences in the spiritual journey. There is a certain level of vulnerability between both the director and directee.

It is for these reasons that I rarely work with the same person as a therapist and as a spiritual director. The orientation of a therapist is counter that of a spiritual director and vice-versa. However, it seemed to me that Marilyn needed some sort-term therapeutic intervention. I suspected that the proper intervention would greatly impact her spiritual life. It turned out that my hunch was right.

At my next meeting with Marilyn, we talked more about her family. Her parents were both well-educated, having graduated college. After their marriage, her mother stayed at home to raise the children and chose not to pursue her career. Marilyn was the oldest, with a brother and a sister. Marilyn's father was well read and encouraged the children in their educational interests. Marilyn was the only one in the family to complete her Ph.D.

I asked Marilyn about her fondest memories with both her father and mother. There were a few stories she shared of holidays and family outings. It seemed to me that her family enjoyed doing things together. I asked Marilyn to describe how her father would encourage her educational pursuits. She spoke of him reading to her as a young child, and later, her telling him about books she read. It sounded like a cozy father/daughter relationship. Yet, as she spoke of talking with her father about reading, school assignments, and other educational endeavors, she became tenser. When I pointed that out, she became more thoughtful.

At first, Marilyn explained that her father always wanted her to do her best. As we continued to talk, Marilyn came to admit that her best was never quite enough for her father. She felt that he always wanted her to do better.

Marilyn and I also spoke about her mother. Her mother kept a bright and cheery home, was always there when Marilyn came home from school, and had dinner ready for the family each evening. Marilyn learned to cook and did many household things with her mother. While Marilyn clearly appreciated the skills her mother imparted, she was equally clear that she was not willing to fulfill the expectations she felt from her parents to be a "good wife and mother" as her own mother had done. As she spoke, it was clear that Marilyn felt angry about what she experienced as expectations to be like her mother.

Over the next few weeks, Marilyn and I explored these parental issues. She was able to recognize that the men she became involved with were very much like her father: they encouraged and stimulated her intellectually but her accomplishments were never sufficient. She felt internal pressure to be a good wife like her mother, to be a happy homemaker and to please her mate. Yet, she was clear in herself that she did not want to be a housewife.

Using hypnosis, I guided Marilyn through a series of exercises. First, Marilyn imagined conversations with each of her parents focused on her feelings regarding her relationship with each parent. This was an opportunity to express the things she had never said. While one can also do this without hypnosis, part of the advantage of using hypnosis is that in a hypnotic state, a person really feels as though he or she is talking to the other person in real life. The emotion can be experienced in a more natural way.

Also in hypnosis, Marilyn was able to enter dialogue with herself as a child and talk to herself about some of the expectations she felt she needed to live up to and temper them with her adult values. Sorting out these childhood feelings proved to be very healing for Marilyn. Through them, she understood that she had been repeating a childhood pattern over and over again in relationship to the men she became involved with. She also was able to come to a sense of resolution with her parents' expectations and separate herself from them. All in all, her parents were the best parents they could be. But in the end, Marilyn needed to live her life by her own decisions, not by those of her parents.

At this point, I moved the focus of Marilyn's attention in another direction. I asked Marilyn what all this had to do with her relationship with God. It didn't take long for Marilyn to realize that she felt as though God was never quite happy with her and that she needed to please God by praying more or doing something better. Her relationship with God had taken on the same characteristics of the relationship she had with her father. Not only had she continued to repeat this pattern with the other men in her life, she repeated the pattern in her relationship with God whom she understood as, "Father." As with the men in her life, she was caught between trying to do what she believed was expected of her and wanting to be her own person. Marilyn was able to sort through the ways her previously unresolved parental issues complicated her relationship with God.

Our images of God are significant for our spiritual growth. It has been said that God first made humanity in the Divine image and since then we have been recreating God in our own image. In many ways, that is true. Often, we project onto God the images that are significant for us. Those images can be both formative and deformative. For instance, the traditional image of God as Father can be profound and healing. A father provides a home and acts out of welfare for his children. A father is kind, generous, and patient. "Father" is an imagine of strength, care, and security. Because few if any of us have had perfect fathers, we easily project onto God the failings of our own fathers. Sometimes, the unresolved hurts we have from our relationships with our fathers, including our feelings about the ways that we may not have met their expectations, are transferred onto God.

It is practically impossible to conceive of God without some image. While God is greater than anything we can imagine, our images are what we can relate to and understand. Our imaginations are often very limited. It's for that reason that spiritual teachers from various traditions encourage people to explore several different images of God. In my own Christian tradition, Jesus spoke of God as a loving Father, a woman who lost a coin, a mother hen gathering her brood, a shepherd who cares for sheep, and an intimate friend. Very simply, aspects of the Divine relationship can be found in every healthy relationship. On the other hand, it's important not to cling too much to just one image of God. For the totality of Divinity cannot be reduced to just one thing. God is Mother, Father, Lover, Friend, Creator, Mother Hen, Eagle, and so much more.

The image of God with which Marilyn was most comfortable was that of Father. Because of this, I encouraged her to explore this image further. Part of this exploration included reflecting and meditating on one of the famous stories Jesus told about God as a loving, generous Father.

This story is found in the fifteenth chapter of the gospel of Luke. The chapter begins with the religious leaders of the day criticizing Jesus for spending time with public sinners. It was their opinion that if Jesus was really a prophet, then he should not be seen with prostitutes, tax collectors, and other people considered undesirable. Jesus' response to their criticism was to tell three stories. The third is the story of the Loving Father.

There was a man who had two sons. The younger one, the one who legally would not inherit anything from his father's estate, said to his father, "Give me my share of the inheritance now, before you die." The father divided the estate equally between the two sons and gave the younger one a share.

The younger son left town for the big city and lost all his money on partying, gambling, and sexual exploits. When he was totally broke, he took the only job he could find: feeding pigs. (Pigs were considered the dirtiest of animals. A religious Jew wouldn't go near a pig, let alone feed one. This young man was living with and feeding a herd of pigs.)

Clearly, he was in a desperate situation. He needed a plan. Knowing that the servants in his father's household had plenty to eat and were a lot more comfortable than the miserable situation he created for himself, he decided to go home. He had it all figured out. He wanted to sound contrite enough to be taken back. He'd ask to live as one of the servants and work the farm. He thought through what he'd say very carefully and rehearsed it till he had it down just right.

In time, he was getting close to home. He was just visible on the horizon when his father saw him. Dad must have been keeping a close eye out for that boy. The father ran to meet him. He threw his arms around his son and kissed him. The boy was shocked. He started his carefully rehearsed speech. While the boy was speaking, the father told the servant to get a clean set of clothes and a ring with the family crest. He told another servant to get everything ready for a party because his son was home. The boy never did give his speech before he was swept into the excitement of the homecoming.

The older son, the one who lost half of what should have been his, the one who stayed home and took care of the place, was out working in a field. He heard the sounds of the party and wondered what all the music and dancing was about. A servant told him that his brother was back and his father was throwing a special dinner. The older son was incensed. How could this happen! That lazy lout is home? A party for him? Clearly, the older son knew that this was wrong. He knew was brother was nothing but a schemer! His younger brother was taking advantage of the naive old man who had lost all sense of judgment.

As the dinner was being served, the father saw that his older son was absent. He went to look for him. The father invited the older son into the party. The older son said, "I've been here with you, taking care of the place, and doing everything I can to be a good son for you. You never even offered to let me invite my friends over for dinner! Yet, that son of yours becomes a public disgrace and you have a fiesta! This is incredible!"

The father lovingly responds to his older son, "Son, everything I have is already yours. You don't have to ask for anything because it's all here for you. But we have to celebrate! Don't you understand? Your brother was dead and he's come back to life! He was lost, but he's found his way!"

The father went back into the party, but the older son, well, the story doesn't tell us what the oldest son did.

This story is usually referred to as the story of the Prodigal Son. It's really not a story about the younger son at all. It's a story about the father who had two very different sons. Despite their differences, the father did all he could to share everything he had with them. It would appear that neither son appreciated the father's generosity. Yet, the generous love of the father was shown to both sons.

In this story, Jesus presents his followers with the image of God as Father. It's an image of generosity, compassion, and acceptance. In the eyes of the father in this story, neither of his sons could do any wrong. Whatever they did, they were welcomed into a party. For both sons, everything the father had was freely shared with them. It is an image of unconditional love.

Marilyn read, studied, prayed with, and reflected on this story. Her image of God as Father grew and changed. She came to understand that the expectations she believed God had of her were meaningless. She realized more of what God's unconditional love meant in her life.

I encouraged Marilyn to imagine herself as each character in the story: the father, the younger brother, the older brother, and the servant who brought the new clothes for the younger son and later told the older son what was going on. She wrote about her reflections in a journal. She took time to see herself in the story and relate each aspect of the story to her own life. In that way she learned to be more accepting of herself for the person she was, tolerant of others' shortcomings, and more generous with her own gifts and abilities.

Part of my work with Marilyn was to help her to discover and affirm a broader and richer relationship with God. It was also to help her understand that she did not have to be limited by the expectations from her past. Instead, she could learn to accept that she already was a lovable and totally acceptable person. There were no expectations she needed to fulfill. Instead, in Marilyn's case, this part of the spiritual path was really a matter of exploring the Divine Affirmation for her and celebrating it.

In time, we spoke more about her relationship with the man she was presently involved with. She quickly understood that things would either have to change in that relationship or that it would end. Her concern about whether or not she should enter a monastic community took on less intensity. She began to understand that what she did was not as important as who she was.

Marilyn came to understand that the formative relationships she had with her parents had a great impact not only on her relationships with men, but also on both her inner struggle to be a unique person and to relate to God as an unconditionally loving Divine Presence. Working past the limitations of the expectations and criticisms she internalized, she was able to enter a new dimension of her relational life, with herself, with the men she dated, and with God.

Marilyn didn't have bad parents. Instead, she had human parents who did the best they could. Yet, Marilyn experienced subtle messages in the ways that both of her parents related to her that she internalized. These messages later caused her difficulty. That happens to many of us. It is also true that these early relationships shape and form our ability to relate to others and to God. So, it's vital for each of us as adults to move past the deformative messages and expectations that we have internalized to be able to grow more fully in every aspect of our lives, including our spiritual lives.

This becomes even more important for those who grew up in harsher environments, where abuse or neglect may have been present. It is very difficult to trust and to have faith in anyone or anything when the early childhood relationships with our parents were marked by the betrayal of our innocence. For some people who were severely abused or neglected, God becomes a savior who protects them in time of trouble. While in some ways that may be a positive image for God, God is more than a "big brother" who rescues us from the bullies in life. Often, until the individual is able to move beyond the childhood pain, God cannot be a trusted friend, a lover, or kind Parent.

About a year after I met Marilyn, she was ready to move beyond our blended relationship of counseling and spiritual direction. The last few months of our work together focused on issues of spiritual direction. I met with her about once a month and was excited to see the relaxed comfort she had in her relationship with God. She came to understand that God was pleased with her just the way she was. Yes, she could continue to grow and be more than she was at the moment. But she could hear the words spoken through the ancient prophet of Israel, Isaiah, as though they were spoken of her: God delights in you and makes you the Divine spouse. (See Isaiah 62:4)

While she continued to date the man she was involved with, she experienced herself as his peer. From what she said, he seemed to adjust rather easily to her critiques of his work, critiques she previously kept to herself.

The progress Marilyn made along her path of personal growth was only partially because she sought out counseling. Psychological counseling enabled her to explore the relationships she had with her family and the repeated patterns of childhood relationships again in her adult life. With this psychological work as a foundation, spiritual direction enabled her to make the connection between her relationships with men and her spiritual life. Because she continued in spiritual direction, regular prayer and meditation, and journaling, she was able to integrate her spiritual life with her relationships and future career. She also was able to begin to live in a more relaxed way. The spiritual work also made the psychological work easier for her because Marilyn was better able to allow the pain stored in her subconscious to surface in meditation so that it could be addressed in a counseling relationship.

Now, Marilyn has sought out a contemplative nun as a spiritual director. She remains interested in monastic spirituality. She understands that her attraction toward monastic spirituality may be something she explores while continuing to teach and date, perhaps as an affiliate to a monastic community. But perhaps, one day, she will choose life in a monastery. Whatever her choice, she now knows it will be her own choice to make. Whether in a monastery or outside of it, she continues to value, explore and develop the spiritual dimension of her life.

Chapter 10

Beginning the Journey along the Good Road

He relayed the story to me as we talked by phone. It had happened a few evenings earlier. At the invitation of a friend, Joe went the meeting of was called a Zen meditation group. Joe and his friend arrived at a house in a residential neighborhood. Below the street number near the door was a small sign marking the house as "the Zen Center." The Center was really the home of the host. A bedroom was converted to a room for meditation.

A total of five people removed their shoes, entered the room and sat on cushions. Incense was lit before an image of the Buddha. A prayer bell was rung at a slow pace. Then silence. Not having received any instructions, Joe sat somewhat nervously in the room. After about ten minutes (yes, Joe was timing it), the leader began to read a portion of the Tibetan **Book of the Dead**. Silence followed. Then another reading. At the end of an hour interwoven with periods of silence and reading from **The Book of the Dead**, the group completed its meditation.

As they left, the leader asked Joe to return. "This will be good for you," the leader insisted. Joe smiled and thanked him. His friend encouraged him too, explaining what an enlightening experience of meditation this was. Joe tried to be polite. But frankly, he thought the whole episode was more than a little bizarre.

As we talked, Joe told me that as a child he used to play along a stream near his parent's home. There, in the woods, he found that he lost himself in nature. "It's like I was a part of it and it was a part of me," he explained. "Yes," I responded. "That is what spirituality is all about."

What Joe experienced in his childhood was the natural, spontaneous experience of spirituality that comes so easily for children. In most cases, children are implicitly taught to ignore these "daydreams" or "flights of fantasy" and be productive in school or the chores assigned to them. Now, at age 29, Joe is working to re-discover the childlike sense of wonder and awe that comes from walking a spiritual path. Like many people, he had hoped in his youth to find that sense of connection and community in Raves and other experiences that promised a communal high. In time, Joe discovered it was not there to be found. Now he is beginning to look for ways to begin walking a spiritual path that are right for him.

Joe is discovering that there are those who are eager to show him *their way* on the spiritual journey. Luckily, he has enough self-awareness to see that *their way* may not be the way that's right for him. He's learning to trust what was true about his childhood experiences and allow his wonder of nature to form the first steps along an adult spiritual path. While he's just beginning, I'm confident he'll find the way that is the path he should follow.

In past generations, most people came to an understanding of the spiritual path through traditions passed on by churches and synagogues. As the role of church and synagogue has changed in society, many people find that institutional religion does little to support their spiritual journey. It would seem that many religious leaders have lost the spiritual wealth that was entrusted to their care. So today, many people attempt to find their own way on a spiritual path. That journey becomes even more confusing in our multicultural, consumer-driven society. Not only do we have access to a variety of spiritual paths and traditions but there are also many self-appointed "teachers" willing to indoctrinate us to their path either for money or to meet their own needs. For Joe and for most people considering a spiritual journey, these are confusing times.

This book is written for people like Joe. In it, I've tried to introduce you to a balanced approach to the basics of the spiritual journey. The early chapters have provided an overview of the dynamics of walking a spiritual path. Exercises were included to assist you to incorporate spiritual practices in your life. The later chapters presented the stories of people at different stages of their spiritual journey to help illustrate what walking the path is actually like. Through it, I've attempted to share some aspects of my own spiritual journey within the context of a balanced understanding of spirituality.

Now, you are left with the opportunity to continue walking a spiritual path. Using the practices contained in this book, you have what you need to begin the spiritual journey. In time, it will be helpful to you to find others who are on a similar journey. But remember: the spiritual journey is much more than just having spiritual experiences. In fact, the spiritual journey is nothing less than the way we live. By cultivating an awareness of the Spirit present in our own lives and in all life around us, we take steps further along the path until the time we find union with the Source of all life. My prayer is that wisdom, strength, and fortitude remain with you as you take the next steps on your spiritual journey. Indeed you will find that it is the good road.

About the Author

Dr. Louis F. Kavar is a professional psychologist, spiritual director, and hypnotherapist in Tucson, AZ. An ordained minister in the United Church of Christ, Dr. Kavar holds 20 years of experience working with individuals and groups in the areas of personal and spiritual development.

Dr. Kavar is director of Desert Vision Center, which specializes in issues of spirituality, wholeness and creativity. He is a faculty member in the Masters in Counseling program at the University of Phoenix, Southern Arizona Campus. He is actively involved in diverse community groups, including the Spiritual Directors Network of Tucson and the Arizona Counselors Association.

Throughout Dr. Kavar's professional career, he has worked with churches, mental health organizations, and other professional groups in areas of spirituality. He has led retreats, taught classes, and presented seminars throughout the United States, Canada, Mexico, England, Australia, and New Zealand. His relaxed manner and use of humor make him an exceptional and accessible presenter in the area of spirituality.

Dr. Kavar holds a Master of Arts from the Institute of Formative Spirituality at Duquesne University, Pittsburgh, in spirituality and a Doctor of Philosophy from the School of Education at the University of

Pittsburgh in counseling. He holds credentials as a Nationally Certified Psychologist from the National Board of Professional Psychologists; a Certified Hypnotherapist from the National Guild of Hypnotists and a Doctoral Addictions Counselor from the National Board of Addictions Examiners.

In addition to several journal articles, Dr. Kavar has published four books: **Pastoral Ministry in the AIDS Era**; **To Celebrate and To Mourn**; **Living with Loss**; and **Families Re-Membered.**

References

Brother Lawrence. (1982). *The Practice of the Presence of God*. Whitaker House.

Dillard, A. (1998). *Pilgrim at Tinker Creek*. Harper Collins.

Bukkyo Dendo Kyokai (Buddhist Promoting Foundation) (1991). *The Teachings of Buddha*. Toppan Printing Co. (S) Pte. Ltd.

Lindbergh, A. M. (1983). *Gift from the Sea: An Answer to the Conflicts in Our Lives*. Vintage Books.

Muto, S. A. (1976). *A Practical Guide To Spiritual Reading*. Dimension Press.

Pennington, M. B. (1980). *Centering Prayer*. Doubleday & Company, Inc.

Progroff, I. (1989). *At a Journal Workshop: The Basic Text and Guide for Using the Intensive Journal*. Dialogue House Library.

Savin, O., Tr. (1996). *The Way of the Pilgrim*. Shambhala Publications, Inc.

Note: Biblical quotations contained in this text are paraphrases and not quotations from any one translation.

9 780595 147175